BE
NOT
DECEIVED

ABOUT THE LAST DAYS

A Bible study commentary on the Scriptures, from Genesis to Revelation, about the certain Second Coming of Jesus Christ in His Glory.

ROBERT BURKE BURNS

CROSSBOOKS
Publishing

CrossBooks™
A Division of LifeWay
1663 Liberty Drive
Bloomington, IN 47403
www.crossbooks.com
Phone: 1-866-879-0502

First published by CrossBooks 6/21/2011

ISBN: 978-1-6150-7852-3 (sc)
ISBN: 978-1-6150-7855-4 (dj)

Library of Congress Control Number: 2011928518

Printed in the United States of America

This book is printed on acid-free paper.

Contents

Preface

As a layperson who loves the study of God's Word I have diligently tried to provide, in this summary study, the reader enough information to encourage a more in-depth look at what the Scriptures teach about the certain Second Coming of Jesus Christ. There are many varied interpretations on this subject, and while I have my own conclusions, it is my hope that the reader will pursue their own convictions about the soon glorious appearing of the Savior, Jesus Christ.

This is not a subject that lends itself to any absolute, dogmatic position. The unfolding over time, and current events, continue to reveal prophetic fulfillments in these last days.

As a pragmatic and literal student of Scripture I began this study to clarify for myself what the Scriptures can tell about the Second Coming of Jesus Christ. Over the years my studies have found much conflicting commentary on this subject, and this research was undertaken to solidify my own understanding and convictions, based on what the Scriptures literally teach.

I have used Scripture to confirm Scripture. When Jesus referenced Old Testament writings, He always spoke of them as true and literal. For many examples read the book of Matthew. In Luke 24:25 He said, *"How foolish you are, and how slow of heart to believe all that the prophets have spoken...".* He literally and accurately fulfilled dozens of prophecies in His First Advent, and there is no reason to not expect the same in Jesus Second Advent.

In church, Sunday school classes, radio/television ministries, internet sites, and books, I have heard and seen some very questionable views and teachings. The lack of studied, in context, whole Bible knowledge is disturbing. It seems the tendency for many is to pick and choose those verses that suit their own position on any subject. Such is the method of deception, either intentional, or through ignorance, prejudice, tradition, and/or lack of serious, in context, Bible study.

American Bible Society President R. Lamar Vest, said, *"The September 28, 2010, research report from The Pew Forum on Religion and Public Life exposes the deficit in religious knowledge among the majority of Americans. Particularly disturbing was the lack of knowledge among self-professed Christians about the Christian faith. Jewish adherents actually had a better awareness of the Bible and Christianity than did the Christians"*.[1]

In this effort I have edited, condensed, commented and summarized, so as to realize the big picture; as seeing the forest and not the trees. Many commentaries are so detailed (as looking at the tree bark) that it is difficult to keep focussed on what the whole body of Scriptures reveal about God's activities and plan for mankind.

For the student there are many details to locate, if that is desired. For me, this broad study put into perspective the whole of God's Word, and helped me come to some personal conclusions about the circumstances of Jesus Second Advent.

Scripture verses are either from the American Standard Version (ASV) of the Bible, as used in my primary reference, "the Second Coming Bible", or from the New International Version (NIV). They are intermixed, depending on the source quoted, or my own use of the NIV in selected verses to complement the study.

Let me encourage the reader to use this study guide commentary as a companion with the Bible version and additional commentaries of choice. (2 Tim 3:16, 17)

May your study efforts bear much witness in these last days,

Robert B. Burns

---

1   American Bible Society Record, Winter, 2011

"Let me therefore beg of thee not to trust to the opinion of any man concerning these things, for so it is great odds but thou shalt be deceived. Much less oughtest thou to rely upon the judgment of the multitude, for so thou shalt certainly be deceived. But search the scriptures thy self & that by frequent reading & constant meditation upon what thou readest, & earnest prayer to God to enlighten thine understanding if thou desirest to find the truth."

"About the Time of the End, a body of men will be raised up who will turn their attention to the Prophecies, and insist upon their literal interpretation, in the midst of much clamor and opposition."

- Sir Isaac Newton (1647 - 1727)

"He (Antichrist) will cause deceit to prosper, and he will consider himself superior." - Daniel 8:25

Introduction

The following pages include references and biographic profiles of some of the more notable Bible scholars that are used in this work. The basic reference was the work done by Dr. W. E. Biederwolf in his personal studies, which are presented in his book, "the Second Coming Bible", published by Baker Book House in 1972. This book is no longer in print from Baker House.

A method of biblical interpretation used in this study is typology, as explained here. Scripture is used to expound and verify other Scriptures.

"Typology is a method of biblical interpretation whereby an element found in the Old Testament is seen to prefigure one found in the New Testament. The initial one is called the *type* and the fulfillment is designated the *antitype*. Either type or antitype may be a person, thing, or event, but often the type is messianic and frequently related to the idea of salvation.

Typological interpretation is specifically the interpretation of the Old Testament based on the fundamental theological unity of the two Testaments whereby something in the Old shadows, prefigures, adumbrates something in the New. Hence, what is interpreted in the Old is not foreign or peculiar or hidden, but arises naturally out of the text due to the relationship of the two Testaments.

The study of types, particularly, types of Christ, is motivated by a number of factors related to New Testament use of the Old Testament. First, the authors of various New Testament books use the Old Testament as a source of pictures pointing forward to Jesus. Among the most obvious passages are 1 Corinthians 10:1-6, Gal. 4:21-31 and the letter to the Hebrews.

From 1 Corinthians, we find Paul using the desert wanderings as typological of the Christian life, while in Galatians, he uses Sarah and Hagar as typological of slavery to Law under the Old Covenant against the freedom of grace in the New Covenant.

The author of Hebrews is concerned to write explaining how the Old Testament points forward to Jesus; in so doing, he draws heavily on Moses the man, as well as the Mosaic Law, with its sacrifices and Temple rituals.

Typology represents a vital part of early Christian hermeneutics* built upon the belief that God is in control and has unified His Word and the events in redemptive history. It is questioned whether typology is prospective (the OT type as a divinely ordained prediction) or retrospective (the NT antitype as analogously related but not prefigured in the type). It is likely that the solution lies in the middle.

The OT writers and participants did not necessarily recognize any typological force in the original, but in the divine plan the early event did anticipate the later reality. Thus David's coronation (e.g., Psalms 2, 72, 110) did indeed foreshadow Jesus' enthronement as the royal Messiah, though it was not a direct prediction.

The term that best describes this balance is "promise-fulfillment". The OT type is promissory and the NT antitype fulfills the divine purpose implicit in the earlier event. Yet there is no need to assert that God had a meaning in the OT type of which the human writer was not aware or that the OT texts had a "fuller sense" or deeper meaning than was realized by the original writers to explain prophetic fulfillment or typology.

A canonical approach to the problem states that any particular biblical text can be interpreted in terms of its total biblical context. In other words, all of Scripture is analogously related, NT writers could see many parallels between Jesus and the religious experiences of Israel (e.g., David's brush with death in Psalms 16:8-11; Acts 2:25-31) without making necessary any "deeper" thrust in the earlier passage."

* Hermeneutics is the science of interpreting what an author has written. In Christian theology, hermeneutics focuses specifically on constructing and discovering the appropriate rules for interpreting the Bible. These methods and principles, however, are often drawn from outside of

scripture in historical, literary or other fields. It inevitably involves exegesis, which is the act of interpreting or explaining the meaning of scripture.

The goal in applying the principles of hermeneutics is to "rightly handle the word of truth" (2 Tim. 2:15), striving to accurately discern the meaning of the text.

-Excerpted from theopedia.com

Primary Reference Used

the SECOND COMING BIBLE, by Dr. William E. Biederwolf
(see biography on next page)

Written in the early 1900's, before World War II, before the 1947 discovery of the Dead Sea Scrolls, and before the establishment of the nation of Israel in 1948. The author confesses to a ministry of over twenty years without a single reference to the coming of the Lord. As a result of his own ignorance he began *"an honest and thorough investigation of the matter at issue. The study was undertaken with no thought of committing the manuscript to the printer."*

In his introduction the author says, *"The work is an impartial study from the standpoint of pure exegesis of such parts of the Old and New Testaments as deal with the glorious appearing of our Lord and Savior Jesus Christ. It has been born out of the author's own experience and has consumed by far the larger part of ten years of his time in the course of its preparation."*

He also stated, *"The work has been prepared not so much with the view of setting forth the author's own conclusions, although this, as a rule, has been done: but with the view of setting forth in popular, plain and concise style the arguments on each side of any portion of Scripture bearing on the subject at hand, where difference of opinion as to its meaning exists, and thus make it possible for every interested reader to intelligently form his own conclusions as to what such Scriptures teach".*

In the preparation of the Scripture testimony he consulted a large number of scholarly interpreters, and quoted from hundreds of them in this book.

Notable Biographies

William Edward Biederwolf (1867 - 1939)

He was born and grew up in Monticello, Indiana. In 1890 he graduated from Wabash College and enrolled at Princeton University, where he graduated in 1894, and then attended Princeton Seminary, from which he graduated in 1895. He later received a fellowship from Princeton to study Greek. For the next two years he also studied at various German universities, following which he toured Palestine. He returned to the U.S. in 1897, married Miss Ida Casad, and was ordained as a Presbyterian minister. His first pastorate was the Broadway Presbyterian Church of Logansport, Indiana.

In 1898 he volunteered for service in the Spanish-American War and was made chaplain of the 161st Indiana Volunteer Infantry. He returned to Logansport for two more years as pastor and resigned to go into full time evangelistic work.

Between 1910 and 1920, he was often listed with noted preachers J. Wilbur Chapman and Billy Sunday as one of the leading evangelists in the country. In 1923 - 1924, he left the U.S. for a preaching tour of the Far East. He served for a time as president of the Interdenominational Association of Evangelists and then as chairman of the Commission on Evangelism of the Federal Council of Churches.

He began the Family Altar League which encouraged members of families to pray and have devotions together. He served as director of the Winona Lake Bible Conference, and also served as director of the Winona School of Theology from 1922 - 1933 and was president from 1933 - 1939. These posts were along with the pastorate of the Royal Poinciana Chapel in Palm Beach, Florida, which he held from 1929 until his death in 1939. He was the author of several books, including the primary commentary source used in this study, "the Second Coming Bible", referenced on the previous page.

- Excerpted from various sources and whitecountyindiana.org/history

Cyrus Ingerson Scofield (1843 - 1921)

American theologian, Presbyterian minister, and writer. During the early twentieth century, his best-selling annotated Bible popularized dispensationalism among fundamentalist Christians. Scofield's correspondence Bible study course was the basis for his popular Reference Bible, an annotated, and widely circulated, study Bible first published in 1909 by Oxford University Press.

Dispensationalism is a Protestant evangelical tradition based on a Biblical hermeneutic that sees a series of chronologically successive "dispensations", or periods in history in which God relates to human beings in different ways under different Biblical Covenants. As a system, dispensationalism is rooted in the writings of John Nelson Darby (1800–1882) and the Brethren Movement. The theology of dispensationalism consists of a distinctive eschatological perspective, as all dispensationalists hold to premillennialism and most hold to a pre-tribulation rapture.

Dispensationalists believe that the nation of Israel is distinct from the Church, and that God has yet to fulfill His promises to national Israel. These promises include the land promises, which in the future result in a millennial kingdom where Jesus Christ, upon His return, will rule the world from Jerusalem for a thousand years. Dispensationalists hold to a wide range of beliefs within the evangelical and fundamentalist spectrum.

Dispensationalism emphasizes the distinctions between the New Testament Church and ancient Israel of the Old Testament. Scofield believed that between creation and the final judgment there were seven distinct eras of God's dealing with man and that these eras were a framework around which the message of the Bible could be explained. It was largely through the influence of Scofield's notes and teachings that dispensationalism and premillennialism became influential among fundamentalist Christians in the United States. He was very influential in the establishment of Dallas Theological Seminary.

Fausset, A. R. (1821 - 1910)

"He studied at Trinity College, Dublin (B.A., 1843), was ordered deacon in 1847, and ordained in 1848, and was curate of Bishop Middleham, Durham, 1847-59. From 1859 he was rector of St. Cuthbert's, York, and was canon of York Munster since 1885. He was chaplain at Bex, Switzerland, in 1870 and at St. Goar on the Rhine in 1873. In theology he belonged to the Evangelical school of the Church of England.

He has written *Scripture and the Prayer Book in Harmony* (London, 1854); *Horse Psalmiece* (1877); *The Englishman's Critical and Expository Cyclopedia* (London; 1878); *The Church and World* (1878); *The Millennium* (1880); *The Signs of the Times* (1881); *Prophecy a Sure Light* (1882); *The Latter Rain* (1883); *True Science Confirming Genesis* (1884); *The Personal Antichrist* (1884); Spiritualism (1885); *Critical and Expository Commentary on the Book of Judges* (1885); and *Guide to the Study of the Book of Common Prayer* (1894).

He edited various classical authors as well as the English translation of J. A. Bengel's *Gnomon Novi Testamenti* (5 vols., Edin burgh, 1857-58), and A. R. Vinet's *Homiletique* (London, 1858), and wrote the second and fourth volumes of *The Critical and Explanatory Pocket Bible* (4 vols. Glasgow, 1862), and the third, fourth and sixth volumes of the *Critical, Explanitory, and Practical Commentary* (6 vols., London, 1871)."

Charles Spurgeon recommended the Jamieson-Fausset-Brown commentary, saying: "Of this I have a very high opinion. It is the joint work of Dr. Jamieson, A. R. Fausset, and Dr. David Brown. It is to some extent a compilation and condensation of other men's thoughts, but it is sufficiently original to claim a place in every minister's library: indeed it contains so great a variety of information that if a man had no other exposition he would find himself at no great loss if he possessed this and used it diligently."
- The above text is quoted from the New Schaff-Herzog Encyclopedia of Religious Knowledge.

Heinrich Friedrich Wilhelm Gesenius (1786 – 1842)

German Protestant theologian and Biblical critic. In 1833, Gesenius published a Latin work, the *Lexicon Manuele Hebraicum et Chaldaicum in Veteris Testamenti Libros*. In 1934 a corresponding issue of the German work, *Hebräisches u. Chaldäisches Handwörterbuch über das Alte Testament*. The *Lexicon Manuele* was subsequently translated to English in America by Edward Robinson D.D. in 1836. The British scholar and theologian Tregelles published his own version in 1846, which was reissued in 1857 with special warnings in a section "To The Student" about scholarly attacks on Christianity and the dangers of Gesenius' rationalism.

The publication of a new Hebrew-English Lexicon was started in 1892 under the editorship of Professors Francis Brown, Samuel Rolles Driver and Charles Augustus Briggs, now well known as the Brown Driver Briggs lexicon or BDB for short. It was published in 1906. With the *Lexicon Manuele* as a starting point, it drew heavily from the *Hebräisches u. Chaldäisches* as well as Gesenius' *Hebrew Grammar* and *Thesaurus*. Since then, both the Tregelles Lexicon and the BDB and have been reissued with Strong's Numbering system.   - Excerpted from 1911encyclopedia.org

Arno Clemens Gaebelein (1861 - 1945)

Methodist minister in the USA. He was also a teacher and a conference speaker. Being a dispensationalist, he was a developer of the movement in its early days. Two of his books, *Revelation, and Analysis and Exposition* and *Current Events in the Light of the Bible* explain the dispensationalist view of eschatology. He also was the editor of *Our Hope*, a Christian periodical, for a number of years, and was a close assistant to Dr. C. I. Scofield on his monumental work, the Scofield Reference Bible.   - wikipedia,org.

G. Campbell Morgan (1863 - 1945)

Born on a farm in Tetbury, England, the son of a Baptist minister. When Campbell was 10 years old, D. L. Moody came to England for the first time, and the effect of his ministry, combined with the dedication of his parents, made such an impression on young Morgan, that at the age of 13, he preached his first sermon. Two years later, he was preaching regularly in country chapels during his Sundays and holidays.

In 1886, at the age of 23, he left the teaching profession, for which he had been trained, and devoted himself to preaching and Bible exposition. He was ordained to the Congregational ministry in 1890. He had no formal training for the ministry, but his devotion to studying of the Bible made him one of the leading Bible teachers in his day. His reputation as preacher and Bible expositor grew throughout England and spread to the United States.

He is noted as a commentator and writer, with numerous publications still available today.   - theopedia.com

R. F. Weidner, D.D., L.L.D. (1851 - 1915)

President of Lutheran Seminary, author, and well respected Bible commentator.

Sir Isaac Newton (1643 – 1727)

English physicist, mathematician, astronomer, natural philosopher, alchemist, and theologian who is considered by many scholars and members of the general public to be one of the most influential people in human history. His studies of the Bible produced a variety of interesting observations.

Newton saw a monotheistic God as the masterful creator whose existence could not be denied in the face of the grandeur of all creation.

Though he is better known for his love of science, the Bible was his greatest passion. He devoted more time to the study of Scripture than to science, and he said, *"I have a fundamental belief in the Bible as the Word of God, written by those who were inspired. I study the Bible daily."*

He spent a great deal of time trying to discover hidden messages in the Bible. After 1690, Newton wrote a number of religious tracts dealing with the literal interpretation of the Bible. The comments below were written by Sir Newton to introduce his studies in Revelation (treatise on Revelation, Section 1.1).

His advice is still relevant today, as we are saturated with many ideas and interpretation of Scripture, and the liberalization of the Gospel.

Sir Isaac Newton continued:

"Let me therefore beg of thee not to trust to the opinion of any man concerning these things, for so it is great odds but thou shalt be deceived. Much less oughtest thou to rely upon the judgment of the multitude, for so thou shalt certainly be deceived. But search the scriptures thy self & that by frequent reading & constant meditation upon what thou readest, & earnest prayer to God to enlighten thine understanding if thou desirest to find the truth.

Which if thou shalt at length attain thou wilt value above all other treasures in the world by reason of the assurance and vigour it will add to thy faith, and steddy satisfaction to thy mind which he onely can know how to estimate who shall experience it. That the benefit which may accrew by understanding the sacred Prophesies & the danger by neglecting them is very great & that the obligation to study them is as great may appear by considering the like case of the Iews at the coming of Christ. For the rules whereby they were to know their Messiah were the prophesies of the old Testament.

And these our Saviour recommended to their consideration in the very beginning of his preaching Luke 4.21: And afterward commanded the study of them for that end saying, Search the scriptures for in them ye think ye have eternall life, and these are they which testify of me: & at another time severely reproved their ignorance herein, saying to them when they required a sign, Ye Hypocrites ye can discern the face of the sky but can ye not discern the signes of the times And after his resurrection he reproved also this ignorance in his disciples, saying unto them, 'O fools & slow of heart to believe all that the Prophets have spoken! Ought not Christ to have suffered these things, & to enter into his glory? And beginning at Moses & all the Prophets he expounded unto them in all the scriptures the things concerning himself.'

Thus also the Apostles & those who in the first ages propagated the gospel urged chiefly these Prophesies and exhorted their hearers to search & see whether all things concerning our saviour ought not to have been as they fell out. And in a word it was the ignorance of the Iews in these Prophesies which caused them to reject their Messiah & by consequence to be not onely captivated by the Romans but to incur eternall damnation. Luke 19. 42, 44."

- *Sources: National Library of Israel, Jerusalem, and* wikipedia.org

Henry Alford (1810-1871)

He was an English churchman, theologian, textual critic, scholar, poet, hymnodist, artist and writer. Before he was ten years of age he had written several Latin odes, a history of the Jews and a series of homiletic outlines. His writings were prolific, and he was a noted lecturer, developing a reputation as scholar and preacher. He published several volumes of his own verse, *The School of Heart* (1835), *The Abbot of Muchelnaye* (1841), *The Greek Testament, The Four Gospels* (1849), and a number of well known hymns.

Alford's chief fame rests on his monumental edition of the New Testament in Greek (4 volumes), which occupied him from 1841 to 1861. Alford's works still provide a quarry where the student can dig with much profit.

- Excerpted from 1911encyclopedia.org

Additional references used

The ***Wycliffe Bible Commentary*** (Moody Press © 1962) is a commentary on the whole Bible written and edited by a large number of scholars representing a wide cross section of American Protestant Christianity. Within the limits of its more than a million and one-quarter words, it attempts to treat the entire text of the Old and New Testaments on a phrase by phrase basis to determine the meaning of the text of Scripture.

Thompson Chain-Reference Bible - New International Version (Zondervan Bible Publishers © 1973), a complete system of Bible study, with chain references, analyses of books, outline studies of characters and unique charts, pictorial maps and archeological discoveries.

And many other commentators and scholars of the Scriptures as found in the commentaries used here, as well as many internet sites and sources.

Preparation for this Study

As preparation for this study it is suggested that first a careful reading of the book of Ephesians is in order. In chapters 1 - 3 the Apostle Paul tells Believers what they are in Jesus Christ. In chapters 4 - 6 he tells Believers what they are to do, how to live their lives, because they are in Christ.

The Believer has responsibility to walk a life worthy of their calling in Jesus, and to engage in warfare against Satan and his hosts (6:11, 12). In this present age the educated Believer can easily see the forces of evil gathering for the last great battle, as the expectation of Jesus Second Coming grows and becomes more evident, as is seen in the world's events of today.

Paul exhorts Believers to *"Put on the full armor of God, so that when the day of evil comes, you may be able to stand your ground...".*

The Old Testament

| **Genesis** | The book of origins, written by Moses. | 1600 BC |
| | The creation: Genesis 1:1; John 1:1, 2. | |

12:1-3   God's covenant with Abraham. His favor and promise to the Jews, and to all families of the earth. Stressed is also the importance of the land.

13:14-18   *"The land"* promised is important. It was *"deeded"* to the Jews *"forever"*.

22:15-18   God's covenant confirmed again, by restating the blessings promised, after Abraham proved his faith.

26:3-24   Covenant confirmed to Isaac. Importance of the *"land and blessings"* stressed.

28:13-15   Covenant confirmed to Jacob. Importance of the *"land and blessings"* stressed.

35:9-12   God appears to Jacob and changes his name to Israel. The *"land"* promised is again stressed as an important part of the covenant.

For almost 4000 years the peoples of Abraham have been given, by God, the promised land of Israel. No power on earth can change that promise. The actual land upon which the nation of Israel sits is very important to God. It's exact location and place in history are of utmost importance to those whom God has chosen as His own children, Jews and Christians alike.

God told Abraham *"I will make of thee a great nation, and I will bless thee, and make thy name great."* All this has happened, and the world is blessed by the Jewish people. Abraham and his descendants would constitute the channel by which God would bless all the peoples of the world. It is from the lineage of Abraham that Jesus came to provide a way of reconciliation between God and rebellious mankind. (Micah 5:2; Matt 1:1, 21)

Leviticus   The book of priestly manner and procedure, written by Moses.   1491 BC

2:11   Rules about leaven, the apt symbol of corruption. A symbol used as a peace offered, uncorrupted (sinless) looking forward to Christ, our sinless offering for our sins.

Chapter 16   The Day of Atonement is a ritual and sacrifice performed by the *"High Priest"*, to accomplish the reconciliation of the nation with God. Hebrews Chapter 9 gives the significance of the ceremony to the Christian. Hebrews 9:28 sums it up: *"So Christ was sacrificed once to take away the sins of many people; and he will appear a second time, not to bear sin, but to bring salvation to those who are waiting for him."* At Jesus Second Coming He will come as the High Priest and Mediator to effect perfect reconciliation with the Father.

Here listed are the Seven Levitical Feasts of Israel and the prophetic significance of each:

1. Passover (Leviticus 23:5) – Pointed to the Messiah as our Passover lamb (1 Corinthians 5:7) whose blood would be shed for our sins. Jesus was crucified on the day of preparation for the Passover at the same hour that the lambs were being slaughtered for the Passover meal that evening.

2. Unleavened Bread (Leviticus 23:6) – Pointed to the Messiah's sinless life (as leaven is a picture of sin in the Bible), making Him the perfect sacrifice for our sins. Jesus' body was in the grave during the first days of this feast, like a kernel of wheat planted and waiting to burst forth as the bread of life.

3. First Fruits (Leviticus 23:10) – Pointed to the Messiah's resurrection as the first fruits of the righteous. Jesus was resurrected on this very day, which is one of the reasons that Paul refers to Him in I Corinthians 15:20 as the "first fruits from the dead."

4. Weeks or Pentecost (Leviticus 23:16) – Occurred fifty days after the beginning of the Feast of Unleavened Bread and pointed to the great harvest of souls and the gift of the Holy Spirit for both Jew and Gentile, who would be brought into the kingdom of God during the Church Age (see Acts 2). The Church was actually established on this

Leviticus

day when God poured out His Holy Spirit and 3,000 Jews responded to Peter's great sermon and his first proclamation of the Gospel.

5. Trumpets (Leviticus 23:24) – The first of the fall feasts. Many believe this day points to the Rapture of the Church when the Messiah Jesus will appear in the heavens as He comes for His bride, the Church. The Rapture is always associated in Scripture with the blowing of a loud trumpet (I Thessalonians 4:13-18 and I Corinthians 15:52).

6. Day of Atonement (Leviticus 23:27) – Many believe this prophetically points to the day of the Second Coming of Jesus when He will return to earth. That will be the Day of Atonement for the Jewish remnant when they "look upon Him whom they have pierced," repent of their sins, and receive Him as their Messiah (Zechariah 12:10 and Romans 11:1-6, 25-36).

7. Tabernacles or Booths (Leviticus 23:34) – Many scholars believe that this feast day points to the Lord's promise that He will again "tabernacle" with His people when He returns to reign over all the world (Micah 4:1-7).

- gotquestions.org

23:34   *"Feast of Tabernacles"* is a memorial to the redemption of Israel out of Egypt. Compare to the Lord's Supper for the Church, *"Do in remembrance of Me"*. This is a memorial to Jesus, and His redemption of the Believer.

26:14-39   The curse for apostasy and contempt of the Law are made by divine threat. As Israel rejected (fell away) from honoring and being obedient to God's commandments and statutes, He set his punishments against the nation, not individuals, for it's apostasy. The judgments are progressive, and embrace the whole of Israel's history. (Isa 3:1-26)

Terror; sickness; loss of power; corrupt leaders; barrenness of the land; plagues of various types; delivery into the hands of the enemy; desolation of the land; and finally, in verses 40-46, upon repentance and obedience, God would remember and again renew this covenant and restoration is promised back to the land.

A prophetic record of what has actually happened to Israel over the centuries, in varying degrees. Now, the Jews are back on their "land", in the new nation of Israel, and awaiting the final and complete restoration at the Second Coming of Jesus, their Messiah.

Numbers   Events in the wilderness. Written by Moses. 1490-1451 BC

24:14-19   Balaam's fourth prophecy foretells the victorious supremacy of Israel over all her foes and the destruction of all the powers of the world. Special reference to the *"latter days"*.

In David the prophecies were partially fulfilled. A wider fulfillment is for the Messiah to finally accomplish in the far distant future, at the time of the end. All of this appears to be a progressive event, culminating in the final completion of the Kingdom of God at the return of our Lord to judgment.

Deuteronomy The words which Moses spake. His farewell, written by
                Moses.   1451 BC

4:26-31   *"Jehovah will scatter you among the peoples and you shall be left few in number among the nations..."* Moses predicts the future dispersions of Israel. Not just an immediate single event, but also the future dispersion under the Romans, which continues, in part, to this very day. Out of these persecutions and sufferings the Jewish people will, *"in the latter days... return to Jehovah"*. A remembrance of the *"covenant"* is declared, and the promise to not destroy them as a chosen people. (Gen 17 and 26:3, 4)

28:64-68   A further foretelling of *"scattering"*. Jews are now found in most every country in the world. *"Among these nations you will find no resting place..."* They are promised a difficult and uncertain life. "How wonderfully and with exact literalness this passage has been fulfilled." - Scofield

Out of their dispersion they will develop a strong desire to have their own nation again, and to reestablish orthodox Jewish worship. To do this they

Deuteronomy

need to rebuild the temple. There are currently plans underway to rebuild the Third Temple on the Temple Mount in Jerusalem.

Reference the following comment by the International Director of the Temple Institute of Jerusalem. See also Ezekiel 37:15-28.

Rabbi Chaim Richman, of the Temple Institute of Jerusalem said on July, 2010, "Tisha B'Av* was not intended to be a day of perpetual mourning, but rather, a bridge to the future; the yearning and desire which our mourning inspires is designed to motivate us to rebuild, ... we hear many excuses, such as who are we to rebuild the Temple? We are not ready. The time has not yet come. The Temple is a thing of the past....The renewal of Israel and the building of the Holy Temple is a process that has begun and is now unstoppable ... This nation is preparing to 'rise up like a lion' (Numbers 23:24). We are moving ever closer to the day on which we can truly say, without jaded cynicism or facetiousness but with true sincerity, that Tisha B'Av is no longer relevant, for it will have turned into a day of gladness."

*Tisha B'av is the day of mourning for the destruction of both ancient Jewish temples: Solomons by the Babylonians, and Herods by the Romans.

- Quoted from various Israel news sources

Chapter 29   A renewed declaration of the original covenant God made with the descendants of Abraham. Moses summons the people to enter again into the covenant, and alludes to the punishments which threaten them in the case of apostasy.

30:1-10   The promise of restoration declared, to the land, and with abundant blessing as they turn to God. *"Jehovah thy God will bring thee into the land which their fathers possessed, and thou shall possess it..."* The passage points to a national and local return, one occurring at a future date. This was only partially fulfilled at the deliverance from Babylonian exile. It seems the final fulfillment of this is happening now. In May, 1948, the nation of Israel was reestablished, and the Jewish homeland is being replanted with it's ancient peoples from all countries of the world. The national conversion of the Jew to his God is not yet complete.

2 Samuel   About the prophet and his times. Writer unknown.

1000 BC

7:8-17, 24, 29   Nathan, the prophet, speaks to David, and tells of God's covenant with David. It is a gradually advancing manifestation of God's favor to David, and for the well being of the people of Israel. Even though history shows disobedience by the Davidic family, and resulting chastisement, the covenant stands. It was renewed to Mary, mother of Jesus, by the angel Gabriel, and as David's earthly throne became extinct, God raised up Christ as his seed to sit on the throne forever. (Luke 1:30-33; Acts 2:29-36)

1 Chronicles   Defines the place of God's chosen people in the world. Writer unknown.

17:7-15   Another confirmation of the Davidic covenant. A promise of future salvation by Messiah, from the line of David. (2 Sam 7:8-17)

Job   Probably written by Moses.   1520 BC

19:25-27   Job's great expression of faith in his future vindication and bodily resurrection. This is one of the most magnificent passages of Scripture. It can be regarded as a prophecy of the Redeemer's Second Coming: *"I know that my Redeemer lives, and that in the end He will stand upon the earth."* Job continues, *"And after my skin has been destroyed, yet in my flesh I will see God; I myself will see Him with my own eyes -- I, and not another. How my heart yearns within me!"*

Psalms   Written by David, and others.   1055 BC

1:5   This verse says, *"the wicked shall not stand (rise) in the judgment"*. The ungodly will not rise at the same time with the righteous. (Rev 20:4, 5)

Psalms

2:1-12   The reign of Jehovah's anointed. In these twelve verses is found the order of the establishment of the kingdom. First, is the worldly rebellion against God and His anointed. As a result there is God's displeasure pronounced by word and deed upon the ungodly nations, and He brings forth His Son, Jesus, and sets Him *"upon my Holy Hill of Zion"*. God promises to *"give thee the nations for thine inheritance"*.

If the nations do not submit they will face *"His wrath"* in the future. The final verse declares, *"Blessed are all they that take refuge in Him"*. (Matt 25:31-34, 41)

8:4-8   Christ's future dominion foretold. The writer ponders as to *"why"* God is *"mindful"* of mankind, and pronounces the visitation of *"the son of man"*, who will be *"crowned with glory and honor"*, who will have *"dominion over the works of thy hands...all things put under His feet"*. (Heb 2:5-11; Rom 8:17-21). Believers are to be joint heirs with Him.

16:9, 10   Christ's resurrection and victory over death and the grave are foretold. (Acts 2:25-32)

22:28-31   The Lord shall rule the nations of the earth. The restoration of the Kingdom of Jehovah. (1 Cor 15:23-25)

24:7-10   The throne of the earth given to the King of Glory. No one is worthy but the Lamb, the King of Glory. (Rev 5:11-13)

41:9   The betrayal of the son of man is foretold, as referenced by Jesus in John 13:18.

45:1-17   Described here is the union and glory of Christ and His triumphant Church. This great Psalm looks forward to the Second Advent in glory.

45:17   Confirms the glory; *"I will make thy name to be remembered in all generations...people will give thee thanks forever and ever."*

Chapter 48   Jewish interpreters take this Psalm to be descriptive of Jerusalem in the Messianic times, after the victory over Gog and Magog.

68:21-35   The King in triumphant ascension and universal dominion. (Eph 4:8)

69:35, 36   These verses declare the rebuilding of the cities of Judah, and the people will dwell there. It is a prophesy now being fulfilled in these last days by the reestablishment of the nation of Israel, and the rebuilding and replanting that is occurring there at this present time.

72:1-20   The reign of Jesus, a glowing description of the reign of Messiah. His reign will be a righteous one (1-7), a universal one (8-11), a beneficent one (12-14), and a perpetual one (15-17). A complete vision of the Millennium Kingdom, which is to be ushered in with Christ's personal return to earth. (Dan 7:13, 14; Rev 5:5-10) All nations shall serve Him.

Chapter 85   A description of God's returning favor when Christ shall establish His government on God's reconciled justice and abounding mercy.

89:1-52   The covenant with David confirmed, and looking forward far beyond David and Solomon. *"I will appoint Him my firstborn...what man can live and not see death?"* No doubt these are foretelling David's line to Messiah Jesus.

Chapters 93 - 99   The rule of Jehovah and the destruction of the unbelieving nations is declared here, and these Psalms constitute a series which celebrate the coming of Jehovah as King, and describing the end of the world and it's final judgment.

102:1-28   The humiliation and the coming glory of the King. Verses 25-27 are in Hebrews 1:11, 12, referring to Christ, so the preceding verses may also.

110:1-7   This Psalm celebrates the exaltation of Christ to the throne of an eternal and increasing Kingdom, and a perpetual priesthood, involving the subjugation of His enemies and the multiplication of His followers. (Matt 22:46; 1 Cor 15:24-28)

Isaiah   Written by Isaiah. Some say another wrote Chapters 40 - 66.   760 - 698 BC

There are two primary divisions of the book: Chapters 1 - 39, looking toward the Assyrian captivity; and Chapters 40 - 66, looking toward

Isaiah

deliverance and future blessing. The writer continually acknowledges the revelations in the book to visions and the spoken word of the Lord.

1:1-24   Jehovahs case against His rebellious and ungrateful people. The rebellion is defined in verses 2-4. In verse 9 a *"very small remnant"* was left by the grace of God. The Apostle Paul calls attention to the failure of Israel to accept the Divine Plan, by rejecting Jesus, in Romans 9:29, and elsewhere. Righteousness cannot be attained by works, only by faith. Just as mere connection of the Jew to Judaism and Israel could not save them from the wrath of a Holy God, so therefore mere connection with the Church also cannot. (Rom 9:30-33; Rom 11)

1:25-31   Zion is to be purged and redeemed. This prophesy is an ongoing fulfillment, and is to be concluded when the Lord comes again *"into His Kingdom"*. *"Justice...righteousness"* is manifest in the destruction of the wicked and deliverance of the *"penitent"* elect.

2:1-5   *"Beat their swords into plowshares"* is a promise to be fulfilled here on this earth when the Lord shall come and appropriate His Kingdom. Then will occur a condition of peace and glory. (Micah 4:1-3; Rev 6:1-17)

2:10-22   On the day of judgment by Jehovah, His terror will be so evident that the *"lofty looks of man shall be brought low, and the haughtiness of men shall be bowed down"*. *"The Day of Jehovah"* is a day of definite *"judgment upon everything"*. (Joel; Amos; 2 Peter 3:8-13)

3:1-26   The judgment of Jehovah pronounced on Jerusalem and Judah because of their prevailing inequities. There is provided here a series of events and conditions that prevailed, a process, if you will, that predicts the outcome as a result of their sin and God's judgments. This process brought about the Babylonian invasion and exile, as well as the Destruction of Jerusalem by the Roman army under the command of Titus, in 70 AD. The conditions that lead to the downfall of the nation:

Verse 1   Lack of food and water,

Verses 2-3   Supports of the state removed,

Verse 4   Government falls into weak and incompetent hands,

Verse 5	Anarchy, insubordination and confusion results from such imbecile rulers,
Verses 6-7	People gladly make a ruler of anyone who has a semblance of sanity and respectability,
Verses 8-9	All these disasters are a result of the peoples own prideful sin,
Verses 10-11	God's judgments that result are not indiscriminate; it will be well with the righteous, but ill with the wicked,
Verses 12-15	The overall result is due to the nations unworthy and corrupt rulers,
Verses 16-24	One of the principal causes of the prevailing evils is expressed as a judgment and punishment of women. The pride, luxury, and extravagant ornamentation of their requirements, plus their outward conduct, results in severe punishment,
Verses 25-26	A disastrous war that causes the loss of life of many men.

It is not a stretch to observe that this process of conditions and judgments run somewhat parallel to what is happening in the USA (and the world governments in general) over the past few decades.

It began in the 1960's with "God is dead", and the rejection of Biblical principles; prayer and the Ten Commandments removed from the public schools and all government locations; and the continuing decline in the morals of the people. Sinful activities have the hearty approval by many governments and peoples; abortion, homosexuality, sexual promiscuity, pornography, etc. There is little moral leadership in government. The people elect self-serving representatives who are corrupt and incompetent. Pride, immorality and materialism reign.

4:2-6   The glorious condition of the future Kingdom is expressed in the deliverance of Israel *"in that day"*, the day of judgment and redemption. The *"glory"* of the Lord will be *"over the whole habitation of Mount Zion"*. This is another possible reference to the necessity of the nation of Israel being in existence and occupying the promised land at the time of this event.

Isaiah

Chapters 5-6   These chapters seem to primarily reference descriptions of the catastrophes that brought foreign powers against Israel, from the Assyrians at that time, to the Romans in 70 AD.

8:9, 10   Israel's enemies *"broken in pieces (shattered)"*. This may look forward to the conspiracy of the Antichrist at the time of the end. (See verse 8, *"O Immanuel"*)

9:1-7   The birth and reign of the King of Peace *"in the latter time"*. A time of spiritual illumination and joy. Verses 6 and 7 are the familiar, *"For unto us a Child is born..."*. The promise of peace, justice and righteousness forever is yet to be performed.

10:20-23   The believing remnant of the Jewish people are to be restored according to the election of grace. (Rom 11:5; Rom 9:27, 28; Zeph 3:12; Zech 12:9, 10)

A *"destruction is determined"* on the majority of the Jewish people then, *"in the latter time"*.

11:1-16   How the Kingdom of David will be established. It begins with *"a shoot out of the stock of Jesse"*, who is, of course, Jesus Christ, the Messiah. (Rev 22:16) *"The spirit of Jehovah"* rests on Jesus, and His judgements will be righteous and just. He will ultimately destroy the Antichrist at His Second Coming. (2 Thess 2:8) Eternal peace and tranquility are foretold: *"for the earth shall be full of the knowledge of Jehovah."* (Jer 31:33, 34)

11:11, 12   The restoration of the Jews *"from the four corners of the earth"* back to the nation of Israel is predicted. It is a regathering of the worldwide dispersion after the 70 AD Destruction of Jerusalem, and it most likely began in earnest in 1948 with the restoration of the new nation of Israel. (Jer 3:18; Ezk 36:10, 37:15-22; Amos 9:15; Ezk 34:28; Isa 60:15, 16, 49:22, 23; Mic 4:1, 2; Zech 8:20-23, 14:16) Both Israel (ten tribes) and Judah are gathered.

Chapter 12   A thanksgiving hymn of the restored and converted Jews. Scofield and others think it belongs to the time of the Millennial Kingdom.

13:1-22   The *"wrath and fierce anger"* of Jehovah is pronounced on the Babylonian empire, and the final overthrow and destruction of Babylon herself. This also most assuredly speaks and applies to judgements to come upon the whole world during the apocalyptic time. (Rev Chapters 6 - 13) The predicted literal destruction of the city of Babylon then existing has been literally fulfilled. The political mystical Babylon of Revelation is also in the prophesy, to be destroyed in the time of the "Beast". (Rev Chapters 17 - 18; Rev 19:19-21)

14:1, 2   Babylon's destruction and Israel's restoration to their own land. Israel's exaltation is to be then, and in a future time.

14:4-23   Primarily a song of triumph by Israel over her fallen enemy, Babylon. Verses 12-23 may be understood as being about the Antichrist who says, *"I will make myself like the Most High"*. The complete destruction and abandonment of Babylon is described in verses 22 and 23.

Chapters 15 - 16   Prophecies concerning the downfall of Moab. 16:15 predicts the throne of Messiah to be established with justice and righteousness.

18:7   In a future time *"gifts will be brought to Mt. Zion"*. (Rev 21:24) This prophecy relates to a future restoration of the Jewish people to their *"place of the Name of the Lord Almighty"*. Jerusalem, Israel. (Isa 66:19)

19:18-25   A prediction of the calling of the Gentiles, that describes the blessing of the Lord on these peoples, specifically some Egyptians and Assyrians. Verses 20 and 21 record prophecies against Egypt, Cush, Babylon, Edom and Arabia that were fulfilled in the past by the conquest of the Medes and Persians. Verse 22 prophesies of the overthrow of Jerusalem by the armies of Sennacherib. Verse 23 is a prophecy against Tyre. A prediction of ruin, then after 70 years a restoration. The complete fulfillment seems to be still in the future.

Preview of Chapters 24 - 27. These are difficult writings to interpret with ease. There are two principal views: These chapters are eschatological and apocalyptic in content, with an Old Testament counterpart in Zechariah Chapters 9 - 14. They are a description of the destruction of the world; the tribulation period during which the Antichrist is revealed. Some commentators maintain that the primary reference of the prophecy is to the coming Babylonian conquest, and it's outcome, with a secondary reference to final times.

Isaiah

24:1-12   The beginning of the judgment. These sobering verses predict a dreadful time on earth as Jehovah delivers harsh judgments because of the sin and rebellion of its inhabitants. *"They that dwell therein are found guilty; therefore the inhabitants of the earth are burned, and few men left."* (Matt 24:6-8; Mark 13:7-8; Luke 21:9; Rev Chapter 6)

24:13-15   The *"few men left"*, the remnant, scattered about the earth. They shall shout and lift up the name of Jehovah, the God of Israel.

24:16-23   The consummation of the judgment is declared, as *"the earth is utterly broken..."*. The punishment from Jehovah on the earth's leaders, *"the kings of the earth, upon the earth"*, may also be the binding of both angelic and worldly powers as prophesied in the New Testament as well. (Rev 20:1-3)

25:1-9   This thanksgiving celebration by Isaiah, praising God for His victory over Israel's oppressors, may be applied to the fall of the world powers then, and the final fulfillment in the end. The great feast celebrates victory over death and the fulfillment of the *"new earth"*, the dwelling place of God with man. (Rev 7:17; 21:4)

26:1-19   The worship and testimony of restored Israel in the days of deliverance of Chapter 25. The resurrection of the dead is brought into view, a triumphant event that causes Israel to praise God. (Hosea 13:14) The dead cannot save themselves, but can only be delivered by God Himself. (Job 19:25, 26) Verse 19 states, *"Thy dead shall live; my dead bodies shall arise...the earth shall cast forth the dead"*. This must reference the literal resurrection at the time of the end. A secondary reference may be made to Ezekiel 37:1-11, as the resurrection of the nation of Israel, fulfilled in May, 1948.

26:20, 21   These are difficult verses to place in time, and there are several valid interpretations presented. God punishes the opposing powers of the world, and takes vengeance on the ungodly. His people are instructed to *"hide thyself for a little moment"*. It seems to reflect on the time in Egypt of the Passover event, where the death angel bypassed those shut in their dwellings with the blood of a lamb on their doorposts (Exodus Chapter 12). God provided escape from His wrath on Egypt, and here is seen His people again placed in a place of safety, as Noah and his family were during the days of the flood judgment. Another possible meaning is that they, God's people, are to remain in the grave until the time of this judgment is passed, then the resurrection. In verse 27, *"Jehovah comes forth out of His place to punish the inhabitants of the earth for their inequity..."*. This view is amplified in Chapter 27.

27:1-11   Jehovah's judgment continues upon the enemies of His people. Several interpretations seek to identify the three sea monsters. They are: A small nation, or several; Egypt, Assyria, and Babylon; Devil, Beast and False Prophet; Satan as the great enemy of the Church.

The restoration of Israel in God's favor shows she, *"shall blossom and bud; and they shall fill the face of the world with fruit"*. Paul alludes to this in Romans 11:11, 12.

27:12, 13   The downfall of Israel's enemies will have the most important consequence: the final restoration of the Jewish people. One interpretation, made long before May, 1948, was as follows: "The Kingdom will be peopled to the fullest extent that had been promised, and that too, as rapidly and as numerous as if human beings were dropping like olives from the beaten trees!" - Gesenius. The land was rapidly repopulated when Israel was reestablished.

The question raised throughout history, after the fall of Jerusalem to the Roman legions lead by Titus in 70 AD, and the subsequent worldwide scattering of the Jewish peoples, was whether or not there would be a literal reestablishment and restoration of Israel, and a repopulation of the land by the Jews. The question was emphatically answered on May 14, 1948.

Since it's founding in 1948 the Jews have rapidly claimed the land, and successfully fought to retain their nationhood. According to the "Jewish Virtual Library" there are about fourteen million Jews in the world in 2010. It is estimated that about forty percent (5,500,000) of the current world's Jewish population now reside in Israel. Another forty percent reside in the U.S.A. About ten percent live in the European Union, with the other ten percent scattered throughout the world.

Chapters 28 - 33   Relate altogether to events of the prophets own day, with a secondary reference to Jehovah's final days judgments. Scofield says, "In these chapters the same blended meanings of near and far fulfillments are found..."

Isaiah

28:14-22 The historical reference is to their dependence on Assyria into which Ahaz had brought them, and the secret alliance with Egypt as well. Neither could save them as God opposed their *"lies...falsehood"* as a refuge. The *"tried stone"* of verse 16 is undoubtedly a reference to Messiah as fulfilled in Jesus.

Of the end time Sir William Blackstone says, "The Antichrist will be received even by the Jews, who have returned to their own land and rebuilt their temple, will make a treaty with him, and called by the prophet Isaiah, *'a covenant with death and an agreement with hell'."* (Verse 15)

29:3-8 These verses reference the invasion and overthrow of the Assyrian hosts against Jerusalem, when the angel of the Lord destroyed Sennacherib's army.

The far view is that of the final gathering of the nations against Jerusalem at the end of the Great Tribulation. Fausset says, "...the ulterior fulfillment of verse 6 in the case of the Jews in the last days may be more literal."

29:17-24 In the days of the Messiah, Israel shall finally realize the moral change that brings the blessings promised by Jehovah. The outpouring of the Spirit in the latter days is referenced.

30:23-33 Blessings are promised to follow Israel's devastation, and Jehovah's burning anger *"sifts the nations with the sieve of destruction...".* Commentators comments: "A description of the Golden Age"; "The glorious time of the end lies beyond the dreadful period which first must be passed through"; "Some great revolution in the state of society"; "Prophecy for the final period of world history." (Rev 20:1-4; Rev 19:17-21)

31:1-9 Warnings against trusting in an alliance with Egypt, that ungodly power. A plea to Israel to place their trust in Jehovah, and return to Him. In modern times we have seen Israel place it's trust in an agreement with Egypt.

The Egyptian leader, Anwar Sadat, lost his life for making it. Israel is still under constant threat from the Arab nations.

32:1-8   The promise of the King with His righteous government is predicted, resulting *"that no longer will the fool be called noble, nor the scoundrel be highly respected"*.

How we long for the day when we can trust government to rule with justice, honesty and respect for the Lord Almighty! When "the scoundrel" is not glorified and held up as an example. When "the fool" is not elected as a representative of the people.

32:14-20   The future glory of Israel is pronounced as a place of security, and a time when *"the Spirit is poured on us from on high, and the desert becomes a fertile field...justice, righteousness and peace will prevail forever"*. The full accomplishment of this Spiritual revival belongs to the Christian dispensation and looks to the time when the Spirit shall be poured on Israel. (Joel 2:28; Acts 2:17; Zech 12:10; Ezk 36:26, 39:29; Micah 5:7)

33:1-24   Primarily considered to be woes upon Assyria and the salvation of Jerusalem. Some commentators relate the invasion and distress to activities by the Antichrist against Christians, and putting a stop to their religious course and conversation. In the present day Christian belief and witness is under attack, and called "hate speech"! (Jude verses 18, 19)

The latter verses indicate a time when *"Jerusalem, a quiet habitation, a tent that shall not be removed...but there Jehovah will be with us in majesty...people that dwell therein shall be forgiven their inequity"*. (Rom 11:25-27)

34:1-4   Judgment on the whole world at the end time. The wrath of Jehovah is *"against all the nations...and their host"*. Utter destruction and slaughter is stated. In addition, *"all the hosts of heaven shall be dissolved..."*. It seems the whole of nature will share in this judgment. The present heaven and earth will be changed. (Rev 21:1)

34:5-15   Judgment on Edom as representing all hostile world powers, as a *"great slaughter in the land of Edom."* It will be a total desolation of the land. The land is scheduled to *"become burning pitch"*. This inextinguishable fire and eternally ascending smoke prove that the final end is being referenced. (Rev 19:3)

34:16, 17   A declaration of the sureness of these prophecies as a promise to possess and dwell in the land of Israel forever.

Isaiah

35:1-10   Israel's redemption and regathering as a people and a nation is prophesied here. Scofield says, "The chapter points to the Kingdom blessing and to the regathering of Israel". Verse 10 declares, *"the ransomed of Jehovah shall return, and come with singing unto Zion; and everlasting joy..."*.

Chapters 36 - 37   Assyria attempts to compel the surrender of Jerusalem, as they had taken all the fenced cities of Judah, but into the city of Jerusalem Jehovah had said to the king of Assyria that he should not come. Sennacherib the king states in 36:20, *"How can the Lord deliver Jerusalem from my hand?"* God's answer is in the following verse!

37:36   The *"angel of the Lord"* slays 185,000 men in the Assyrian encampment in one night. The Assyrian army and king depart to Nineveh, where Sennacherib is slain by two of his sons.

Chapters 38 - 39   King Hezekiah's sickness and recovery as a result of his prayer of faithfulness. God provides a miraculous sign by moving the sun backwards! In 39:6 Hezekiah is told by Isaiah that a day is coming when all the treasures of his palace *"will be carried off to Babylon"*. The prophecy was literally fulfilled, and proved God's power and judgments.

Chapters 40 - 48   These chapters present the absolute power and wisdom of God, and the redemption he offers to all humanity.

40:6-8   The glory of man is short-lived, just as the *"grass withers and the flowers fall,* but *"the word of our God stands forever"*.

Chapter 41   God's *"chosen"* servants are seen as the Helpers of Israel. His plan and protection of Israel as a people, and a nation, is declared. *"I, the God of Israel, will not forsake them."*

Chapter 42   The Messiah is introduced, who as the personal representative of a new covenant will mediate for all nations, especially Israel. In verses 6-9 this new covenant and promise of redemption is declared. Scofield, and others, see in this chapter the two fold account of the coming of Messiah. His first in mercy to the repentant, and His second in judgment on His enemies.

Chapter 43   This chapter focusses on the promise of Israel's redemption, in spite of all difficulties. In verses 10-12 the Lord declares His purpose for Israel: *"You are my witnesses, and my servant whom I have chosen, so that you may know and believe Me... You are my witnesses, declares the Lord, that I am God."*

Chapter 44   *"Israel, whom I have chosen"* is the continuing subject. God promised to *"pour out my Spirit on your offspring, and my blessings on your descendants"*. He condemns idols, and ridicules what they are...manmade and detestable: *"they know nothing...shall I bow down to a block of wood?"* In verse 28 is a specific prophecy about Cyrus, and what God will use him for in the future restoration of Jerusalem after the Babylonian captivity.

Chapter 45   Here is set forth the deeds of Cyrus as God's chosen instrument in the restoration and salvation of Israel at that time. The Lord proclaims a final and future salvation for Israel that will be *"an everlasting salvation."* All of God's enemies will be *"put to shame"*, and *"before Me every knee will bow...".*

Chapter 46   The gods of Babylon are ridiculed, and the house of Israel is challenged to compare Jehovah to them. *"I am God, and there is none like Me. I make known the end times from the beginning, from ancient times, what is still to come."* (Luke 24:25)

Chapter 47   The downfall of Babylon is the subject. *"Disaster... calamity...catastrophe"* are prophesied to come upon Babylon, as they *"showed no mercy"* on the captive Israelites. The Babylonian *"astrologers... those stargazers who make predictions month by month"* are challenged to *"save you"*. They have no power to save anyone.

Chapter 48   Israel's, specifically Judah's, stubbornness is challenged to understand what the Lord Almighty says comes to pass: *"then suddenly I acted"* was a fulfillment of *"I told you these things long ago"*. What is prophesied by God's chosen prophets is sure to be literally fulfilled. (1 Thess 5:20; 2 Pet 1:17-21) A *"new thing"* (verse 6) is declared about God's purpose against Babylon, and the redemption to come for *"Jacob"* (verse 20). The redemption of Israel began with the exodus from Egypt (verse 21) and is yet to be completed (verse 22).

49:6   The restoration of Israel and the calling of the Gentiles. Implied is also that Israel shall be restored according to it's original distribution into twelve tribes. (Rev 7:4)

Isaiah

49:8-12   The Lord promises *"to restore the land"* and to call His people back for the restoration of Israel. It begins with the deliverance from Babylonian captivity and ends with the completion of salvation in the world beyond.

49:17-26   Desolate Israel is built again with Gentile help. The Gentiles shall aid in restoring Israel to her own land, therefore this must refer to the literal restoration of Israel. Numerous commentators of old understood that in the last days the literal nation of Israel must be back on the land for which God declared His love. The return of Jesus could not occur before the fulfillment of these prophecies about the reestablishment of the nation of Israel. * How perfectly the prophecies in God's Word are fulfilled!

> * Refer to the following information regarding the Balfour Declaration in 1917, done with Gentile help!

The Balfour Declaration of 1917 (dated 2 November 1917) was a formal statement of policy by the British government stating that:

"His Majesty's government view with favour the establishment in Palestine of a national home for the Jewish people, and will use their best endeavours to facilitate the achievement of this object, it being clearly understood that nothing shall be done which may prejudice the civil and religious rights of existing non-Jewish communities in Palestine, or the rights and political status enjoyed by Jews in any other country."

The declaration was made in a letter from Foreign Secretary Arthur James Balfour to Baron Rothschild (Walter Rothschild, 2nd Baron Rothschild), a leader of the British Jewish community, for transmission to the Zionist Federation of Great Britain and Ireland, a Zionist organization. The letter reflected the position of the British Cabinet, as agreed upon in a meeting on 31 October 1917. It further stated that the declaration is a sign of *"sympathy with Jewish Zionist aspirations."*

The statement was issued through the efforts of Chaim Weizmann and Nahum Sokolow, the principal Zionist leaders based in London; as they had asked for the reconstitution of Palestine as "the" Jewish national home, the declaration fell short of Zionist expectations.

The "Balfour Declaration" was later incorporated into the Sevres Peace Treaty with Turkey and the Mandate for Palestine. The original document is kept at the British Library.

The anniversary of the declaration, 2 November, is widely commemorated in Israel and among Jews in the Jewish diaspora as Balfour Day. This day is also observed as a day of mourning in Arab countries still today.

The declaration, a typed letter signed in ink by Balfour, reads as follows:

Foreign Office, November 2nd, 1917.
Dear Lord Rothschild,
I have much pleasure in conveying to you, on behalf of His Majesty's Government, the following declaration of sympathy with Jewish Zionist aspirations which has been submitted to, and approved by, the Cabinet:
"His Majesty's Government view with favour the establishment in Palestine of a national home for the Jewish people, and will use their best endeavours to facilitate the achievement of this object, it being clearly understood that nothing shall be done which may prejudice the civil and religious rights of existing non-Jewish communities in Palestine, or the rights and political status enjoyed by Jews in any other country".
I should be grateful if you would bring this declaration to the knowledge of the Zionist Federation.
*   Yours sincerely,*
*   Arthur James Balfour*   - wikipedia.org

Chapter 51   The promised redemption of Israel and their return for a future of *"everlasting joy"*. Some commentators see the coming oppression by Antichrist and the desperation of those times in the latter verse of this chapter.

Chapter 52   The restoration of Jerusalem to glory. Christ is prophesied as the suffering servant, highly exalted. A vivid description of the brutality of His suffering is provided (verse 14).

Chapter 53   Portrays the humiliation and suffering of the *"man of sorrows"*. A vivid prophesy of the coming Messiah, fulfilled by Jesus some 700 years later.

Isaiah

Chapter 54   Sets forth the future glory of Zion, and the joyful salvation of Jehovah's people. The prophet describes the security and blessings of the restored nation.

"Seek the Lord" is the theme of Chapter 55, as a universal invitation to God's freely given salvation. *"Turn to the Lord and He will have mercy... he will freely pardon"*, - verse 7. The Lord declares that man cannot fully understand His thoughts, and His ways, which are purposed to accomplish that which God desires. His plan is in His complete control.

Chapter 56   Describes a series of ethical instructions and the resulting blessings of good behavior. Some aspects point to a future fulfillment, probably in the Millennium Age.

Chapter 57   Begins with the condemnation of rebellion and idol worship during Israel's exile in Babylon. Even so, a believing remnant will be graciously cared for and return to *"inherit the land and possess my holy mountain"*. A literal repossession of the land is foretold.

The prophet provides guidance in Chapter 58 for true repentance and true fasting, as contrasted with false worship.

58:12   The verse specifically declares the rebuilding and repair of *"ancient ruins"* by the Jewish people. A restored Israel is in view here.

59:15-21   The promise of Jehovah's intervention and judgment because His people were so corrupt. *"It displeased Him that there was no justice...no intercessor"*. No one to atone for the unrighteousness of the people. Verses 18-19 show a universal judgment on the world of nations with an overwhelming victory over Jehovah's enemies. The final two verses declare the time when the Redeemer shall come to Zion following the completion of the Gentile Church. Paul references this in Romans 11:23-29. Also see Acts 15:14-17.

60:1-9   The gathering of the nations to Jerusalem as the glory of Jehovah's spiritual light shines forth. Israel has been restored to the land and the Second Coming has occurred as Israel takes her true position as mother of the Church. Verse 7 has caused great dispute among commentators. Is it calling for a literal or spiritual restoration of Israel and temple sacrifice?

It seems clear today that a literal explanation is in order. Israel is a nation again, and grand plans are underway to rebuild the temple and reinstitute animal sacrifice. Verse 9 can easily be seen as predictive of the great 1947 - 1948 exodus of Jews back to the land, by ships from many nations.

60:10-16   The restoration of Jerusalem and the resulting glory that will be fulfilled after the Second Coming. Jerusalem is the place Jehovah has chosen to dwell with His people forever. It will be a beautiful and glorious sanctuary that is known as *"the city of the Lord"*. (Rev 21:9-27)

60:17-22   The New Jerusalem will be a place where peace and righteousness rule. (Rev 21:23-27) These verses portray a place of *"everlasting light...no sorrow...all the people righteous, and they will possess the land forever"*. God proclaims them as *"the work of my hands for the display of my splendor...in its time I will do this swiftly"*. When God decides to act, it will be sudden and complete. See comments on Luke 17:22-37.

61:1-11   The speaker in these verses may be Messiah. Jesus suspended the reading of this passage in the synagogue at the comma in the middle of verse 2. (Luke 4:17-21) The First Advent opened the day of grace. The *"day of vengeance of our God"* will be taken up when Jesus returns. Verse 1 declares the preaching of *"good tidings unto the meek...to proclaim liberty..."*. Proclaiming liberty refers to the deliverance from the bondage of sin. The following verses describe the glory of a saved Israel in the Millennium, and the Gentiles provision for their needs. (Rom 15:27)

62:1-12   Messiah continues to speak about the development of the glory of Jerusalem. He continues to work on behalf of His people, calling them to righteousness and salvation. Implied here is the last days restoration of the people, and that Jerusalem shall no longer be abandoned, but highly prized and loved. The Second Coming of Jesus is in view in verses 11 and 12.

63:1-6   Messiah is here pictured as approaching Jerusalem after the judgment of the end time upon the Antichrist. *"I have trodden the winepress alone..."*, indicates this is the wrath of God's judgment on all enemies, unattended by any assistance from man. (Rev 14:20; 19:13-15; 19:18-21)

63:7-19   The prophet now offers thanksgiving, confession and supplication for Jehovah's people, especially relating to the future restoration of Israel. He reminds the people of the kindness of the Lord,

Isaiah

and that God is not their adversary. In verse 15 Jehovah is called upon to *"look down from heaven and see..."*. Here begins the prophet's fervent appeal to God to pity Israel now on the ground of His former mercies to them, an appeal which continues throughout Chapter 64. It is a plea to end Israel's distress and *"to come down to make your Name known to your enemies..."*. Jehovah's answer to the prayer of the people is recorded in Chapter 65.

65:1-7   Not all Israel shall be saved, as destruction and not salvation awaits a larger portion of the nation. Gentiles may also be referenced here, as *"a nation that was not called by my Name"*.

Descriptions of idolatrous abominations call for God's wrath and punishment, which will be done as *"full payment for their former deeds"*. (Jer 22:30; Rom 10:20; Zech 13:7-9)

65:8-16   Not all Israel is cast out, as a remnant is to be saved according to the election of grace (Rom 11:28). They shall be restored to an occupation of the whole of Palestine.

65:17-25   The promise of eternal blessings to the remnant and the whole earth creates *"new heavens and new earth...former things will not be remembered"*. This predicts the change coming in the existing state of things that looks beyond this present age to the renovation of the whole earth which shall come at the end time. (Rev 21:1)

Before this time predicted, will be a time (Millennium) far superior to those of the present, but it will not be perfect, as sin and death will still exist (Rev 20:7, 8). Death, the last enemy, is not destroyed until after Satan's rebellion at the end of the Millennium (Rev 20:14).

66:1-14   The rebirth of Israel and the condition of things expected in the time of the end when there will be a new heaven and a new earth. Implied is the promise of a rebuilt temple, either Herod's temple at the time of Jesus, or in the future new Jerusalem (Chapters 56 and 60).

Verse 6 commentaries offer many explanations, but the most satisfactory shows Jehovah's judgment going forth from the temple which has risen again. Verses 7 and 8 expresses the sudden and unexpected reproduction of the Jewish nation in their own land in the latter days.

Israel was reborn as a nation in one day; May 14, 1948. In the war of 1967 Jerusalem was captured by the Jews. Reference Jeremiah 39:7 and the "Six Day War".

66:15-24   After Israel is restored to their land these verses paint a general picture of the time of the end. The great *"anger with fury"* is the wrath of God when he *"executes judgment on all men"*. This is a judgment with *"fire...flames of fire...fire with His sword"*. The book of Isaiah closes with the terrible condition of those who rebelled against God. The future of the wicked is eternal damnation. (Rev 20:15)

During this period of final judgment (the wrath of God), the godly Believers will be hidden away. Reference 1 Thess 4:13, 5:9; 2 Thess 2:1-8; Matt 24:15, 30-31; Dan 7:13, 14. Exactly how and when this *"hiding away"* transpires is subject to numerous interpretations.

There is a remnant spared (verse 19) and a *"sign"* given. A variety of commentaries offer explanations, but none are completely satisfactory. Some are elected to survive this time of judgment and seem assigned to preach the Gospel to certain nations and peoples. *"They will proclaim my glory to the nations."* Could this be the 144,000 sealed of Revelation Chapter 7? Zech 14:16 states, *"then the survivors of all the nations that have attacked Jerusalem will go up year after year to worship the King, the Lord Almighty, and celebrate the Feast of Tabernacles."*

Jerusalem will be the earthly center and home of Jehovah. The thousand year reign of Christ will commence (Rev 20:4).

Jeremiah   Written by the Prophet Jeremiah.   629 - 588 BC

1:4,5   The call of Jeremiah is a declaration of God's work of plans and appointments for His chosen representatives. Jeremiah was chosen before being formed in the womb. *"Before you were born I set you apart..."* Jeremiah recorded 30 - 40 years of prophesy, history and information.

2:7   There is no doubt God has a special interest and claim on the Jews promised land. *"You came and defiled My Land..."*

Jeremiah

2:21   God condemns His people for their sin of forsaking Him and turning to idols. They had *"turned against Me into a corrupt, wild vine..."*

2:28   Depending on *"the gods you made for yourselves, let them come if they can save you..."* is a pronouncement on the worthlessness of idol worship.

3:14-18   The promise of a final restoration and blessing to the Jews. These verses no doubt contain an allusion to the final period. The future restored Israel is to be a numerous people, with *"Jerusalem, the throne of the Lord"*. The reuniting of Judah and that of Israel are foretold, as a literal event, awaiting fulfillment in the end times (50:4-7).

Chapters 4 - 11 Are a detailed condemnation on the Jews for their unfaithfulness and covenant breaking sins. Their defeat and captivity by the Babylonians is predicted.

12:14-17   Obedience to be rewarded by a final reunion with Jehovah. The carrying away of Judah by the Babylonians also included her neighbors, the Gentile nations. They all were carried away into exile by Nebuchadnezzar. Verse 16 offers a challenge to the nations exiled to *"learn well the ways of My people..."*, to learn about the Lord and become established, rather than destroyed as stated in verse 17.

16:14,15   Future restoration promised is primarily from Babylonian captivity. Campbell Morgan comments expand this promise as a restoration from a worldwide dispersion back to the land of Palestine, which at the time he wrote it was then unfilled. Since 1948, Jews from all over the world continue to resettle the new nation of Israel.

Chapter 20   Jeremiah expresses his sorrow for ever being born, as he is *"ridiculed all day long; everyone mocks me..."*. As a prophet of the Lord his task of telling people of their sin, unfaithfulness and idolatry is a tremendous burden. His warnings of impending destruction and captivity are ignored. So it also is today! See 2 Peter 3:3, 4.

23:1-8   The future restoration and conversion of Israel is predicted. The "ten lost tribes" were carried away captive into Assyria in 725 BC. To this day their whereabouts is known only to God. Judah was carried away captive into Babylon in 588 BC. They began returning to the land about 70 years later, and restored the temple and occupation until being finally scattered in 70 AD by the Romans.

The final restoration *"out of all countries"* is now in the process of being fulfilled, as the nation of Israel of modern times struggles to survive. So far the Jews have not yet enjoyed the temporal blessings foretold in verses 6 - 8, as a result of Messiah's reign. This accomplishment will occur after the Second Coming of Messiah Jesus. (Jer 16:14, 15; 33:15, 16)

23:20   Jehovah's unalterable purpose as to Israel and her enemies will be fully revealed *"in the latter days you will understand it perfectly"*. (Hosea 3:4, 5)

24:4-7   The promise of a future restoration and conversion of the exiled Jews of Judah. Here the Lord separates the *"good figs from the bad figs"*, and promised to *"give them a heart to know Me"*.

Chapter 25   Is devoted to the prophecy of the seventy years captivity in Babylon because of their disobedience (verse 7). At the end of the seventy years deliverance was to come and judgment on all the nations in that known world. *"Seventy years"* seems to be a *"time of fulfillment"* by God as He does His work in completing prophecies. Refer to Daniel's "Seventy Weeks" as well.

25:29-38   These verses predict and define the final judicial act of God in it's last and highest stage. This judgment is on all nations of the earth, absolutely without regard. *"He will bring judgment on all mankind and put the wicked to the sword"* (verse 31). This is the *"Day of the Lord"*. (Isa 2:10-22; Rev 19:11-21; Rev 16:14) It is *"the wrath of God"*. (2 Thess 1:6-10; 1 Thess 5:9; Matt 24:21-31; Isa 24)

29:12-14   A renewal of the promises of Deut 30:1-10, that Israel is to be regathered to her original place *"from all the nations"*. This was included in the *"text of the letter that the prophet Jeremiah sent to the surviving elders among the exiles..."*. A period of seventy years was established as a time frame of completion (verse 10).

30:1-24   Israel in tribulation and the promised deliverance prophesied here may primarily look to the restoration of the Jews from Babylon, but also must look further on into the future.

Jeremiah

Verse 7 says of the time of tribulation concerning Judah, *"Alas! For that day is great, so that none is like it..."*. Verse 11 says, *"I will make a full end of all the nations where I have scattered you; but, I will not make a full end of you..."*. It is the time of *"Jacob's trouble"*. (Matt 24:22; Joel 2:11, 31; Amos 5:18, 19; Zeph 1:14, 15; Rev 6:17)

The promised future restoration comes through *"their leader...their ruler"*, who must be Messiah, the Christ. The chapter concludes with the admonition that the Lord's wrath and purposes will be understood *"in days to come"*.

31:1-40   The love of God for all Israel and Judah is decreed, as a full restoration and new covenant. This occurs in the time of the latter days and is, as yet, unfulfilled. A universal restoration to the home land of all manner of peoples is promised in verses 8 and 9. A new covenant is predicted in verses 33, 34. (Hebrews 8:7-13) The knowledge of the Lord will be universal as the teaching of the Holy Spirit indwells the hearts and minds of the people. The external city of Jerusalem is to be completely rebuilt and made holy for this completion of the Kingdom of God on earth.

Chapter 33   Is a reaffirmation of the promises and power of Jehovah to fulfill the promise of Israel's glorious future. In verses 15-18 the *"righteous branch sprout from David's line"*, is predicted. Messiah's literal priesthood, and His followers spiritual priesthood and sacrifices shall never cease. (Heb 7:17, 21, 25-28; Rom 12:1, 15:16; 1 Pet 2:5, 9; Rev 1:6)

39:7   The beginning of the *"times of the Gentiles"*. King Zedekiah's eyes were put out by the Babylonians (52:10, 11), and he was bound with chains and taken to Babylon. Since that time until June, 1967, Jerusalem had been under complete Gentile rule and domination. That changed as a result of the Six-Day War.

The Six-Day War or June War, also known as the 1967 Arab-Israeli War or the Third Arab-Israeli War, was fought between June 5 and June 10, 1967, by Israel and the neighboring states of Egypt [known then as the United Arab Republic (UAR)], Jordan and Syria. At the war's end,

Israel had seized the Gaza Strip and the Sinai Peninsula from Egypt, the West Bank and East Jerusalem from Jordan, and the Golan Heights from Syria.

The judgment of the Gentiles and deliverance of Israel is recorded in the vision of Chapter 46. Scofield calls attention to the fact that we are to distinguish between a near and far fulfillment of these prophecies against the Gentile nations. Verses 27-28 look forward to the judgment of the nations after Armageddon (Matt 25:32) and the deliverance of Israel. Reference Chapter 30.

48:46,47   The conversion of the heathen in the final period in Messianic times. Similar promises are made for Egypt (46:26) and for Ammon (49:6) and Elam.

50:4-7   The chosen people restored and united in eternal covenant with God. Israel and Judah will, in a future time, be gathered together and *"bind themselves to the Lord in an everlasting covenant..."*. (Zech 12:10-13)

51:59-64   The final words of Jeremiah as he was in Babylon with King Zedekiah. The prophesies about the future fall and desolation of Babylon were written on a scroll, to be read aloud to the people. Then the scroll was to be *"tied to a stone and thrown in the River Euphrates"*. The prophesied desolation of that city Babylon, have been fulfilled.

Chapter 52   Closes the book with a detailed summary of the events concerning the fall of Jerusalem and the captivity of Judah taken into exile by Nebuchadnezzar.

Ezekiel   Written by the Prophet Ezekiel.   595 BC - 574 BC

Chapters 1 - 3 Ezekiel encounters the Lord through a most unusual and unexplainable vision. The mystery of it all only enhances his call as a prophet and deliverer of messages to the Israelites, *"a rebellious nation that has rebelled against Me..."* (2:3, 4). The hardheaded stubbornness of the Jewish people as a whole has not yet been relieved.

Ezekiel

on May 14, 1948. Many commentators believe this to be a fulfillment of this passage of Scripture, and many other prophecies in this regard. The formation of the Jewish State after almost 2000 years is a testimony to the literalness of prophecy.

Formation of the Jewish State.

On May 14 (because the 15th was the Jewish Sabbath), one day before the scheduled date of British withdrawal and the expiration of the British Mandate, the Jewish community in Palestine published a Declaration of Independence as the State of Israel and announced the formal establishment of the provisional government. The UN Resolution is mentioned in the Declaration of Independence as recognizing the right of the Jewish people to establish a state. In accordance with the UN Resolution, the Declaration also promised that the State of Israel would ensure complete equality of social and political rights to all its inhabitants irrespective of religion, race or sex, and guaranteed freedom of religion, conscience, language, education and culture.   -wikipedia.org

---

37:15-28   The reunited tribes are restored to their land. Scofield says, "We have here a promise that the ten and two tribes shall no longer be divided into two kingdoms, and that the earthly center of the worship of God shall be in Jerusalem." The final process of the restoration and salvation of the Jewish people began with the reborn Israel established in the promised land. As the end of days approach the literal interpretation of all these prophecies and promises is expected. Messiah will come to fully restore the Jewish nation to Palestine, reestablish the Kingdom of David, rebuild the temple and institute the sacrificial worship of the Levitical Law. Many of the deepest students of Scripture believe this, with variation.

Jewish plans to rebuild the temple in Jerusalem and reinstitute the sacrifices are a major effort at this present time. (See also Matthew 24:16) Wycliffe comments, "This prophecy, like the preceding one, has not yet been fulfilled historically, for so far, Israel has failed to meet the conditions. Its fulfillment lies in the future ingathering of a converted Israel into the body of Christ. It looks forward to the time when the Tabernacle of God will be with His people (Rev 21:3)."

The Temple Institute in Jerusalem is an organization in Israel focusing on the controversial endeavor of establishing the Third Temple. It's long-term aims are to build the Third Jewish Temple on the Temple Mount, on the site currently occupied by the Moslem "Dome of the Rock", and to reinstate sacrificial worship. The Institute aspires to reach this goal through the study of Temple construction and ritual and through the development of actual Temple ritual objects, garments, and building plans suitable for immediate use in the event conditions permit its reconstruction. The International Department is headed by Rabbi Chaim Richman.
Reference also Deuteronomy 28:64 - 68.   - wikipedia.org

Chapters 38 - 39   These chapters paint a vivid panorama of the *"latter days"* invasion of the land of a restored Israel. This invasion is by a confederacy of nations lead by *"Gog"*. This powerful army of many nations, intent on *"plundering"* (see U.S. Govt. report below) Israel, dwelling in security with *"unwalled villages"*, will be destroyed by the wrathful judgment of God. The details revealed indicate an unimaginable slaughter of the enemies of God.

Most commentators today see these prophesies as being literally fulfilled, either in completeness, or in some variation of detail.

Before Israel's recent rebirth as a nation, and the development of Russia as a world power, plus some Middle East nations becoming more friendly with Russia, some commentators viewed these passages as only a spiritual struggle. Now current world events seem to strongly indicate a literal coming fulfillment of this terrible war.

U.S. GOVERNMENT REPORT: ISRAEL HAS 122 TRILLION CUBIC FEET OF NATURAL GAS OFFSHORE, AND 1.7 BILLION BARRELS OF RECOVERABLE OIL.

Ezekiel

A recently-released report (May, 2010) by the U.S. Department of Interior, U.S. Geological Survey, indicates that Israel has massive reserves of natural gas and oil supplies just offshore, lying under the Mediterranean. "The *U.S. Geological Survey* estimated a mean 1.7 billion barrels of recoverable oil and a mean of 122 trillion cubic feet of natural gas in the Levant Basin Province using a geology based assessment methodology," stated the report's executive summary.

Israelis for years have lamented that if God wanted to bless them with a "promised land" He could have given them the oil-rich Arabian peninsula. Thus the report has become big news in the Israeli media and the energy industry. Several oil and gas companies are already at work there and have made more modest discoveries in recent years. But this is by far the biggest development to date and some reports indicate Israel could begin using the natural gas — and possibly exporting it — within two years.

- Source: U.S. Department of the Interior, U.S. Geological Survey

---

38:1-23   The destruction of Gog and his great army of nations is revealed in these verses. Gog refers to an individual ruler (39:1), as the leader of the army of nations, primarily from the *"uttermost parts of the north"*. The identity of these nations primarily includes those living at the extreme north, east and south borders of the then known world. Today this would include Russia, Turkey, Syria, Iraq, Iran, Jordan, Libya, Lebanon, Egypt, Saudi Arabia, and some others of the former Soviet Union, eastern Europe and north Africa. Many of these nations are under Islamic control. The exact identity of the nations to be involved is yet to be determined.

Current events find unprecedented alliances being made between Russia, Iran, Turkey and others. In verse 8 is found the time of occurrence, *"in the latter years"*, and the place of occurrence, *"upon the mountains of Israel"*. (Rev 19:11-21)

In Revelation 20:8 is also found a time frame for the final destruction of *"Gog and Magog"*, and that is at the end of the Millennium, when *"Satan is loosed"* for a time to *"deceive the nations which are in the four corners of the earth"*. This seems to be a separate occasion, although alluded to in Ezekiel. This final struggle with the enemies of God , lead by Satan, will be brief and fierce. The result will be the fulfillment of all prophesy, and *"a new heaven and a new earth"* (Rev Chapter 21), created after the final judgment (Rev 20:11-15).

39:1-29   The judgment on Gog and his army is given more detail. The completion of this divine judgment is the complete annihilation of the enemy. The slaughter will so extensive so as to take years to *"cleanse the land"*. It is concluded that this conflict is to be on this earth.

Scofield says, "The primary reference is to the Northern European powers, headed up by Russia, all agree. The whole passage should be read in connection with: Zechariah 12:1-4, 14:1-9; Matthew 24:14-30; Revelation 14:14-20, 19:17-21."

"The prophecy belongs to the yet future 'day of Jehovah', and to the battle of Armageddon, but includes also the final revolt of the nations at the close of this age."

According to Gaebelein, "The invasion which Ezekiel describes takes place at the beginning of the Millennium (or the end of the Great Tribulation), whereas the invasion of Gog and Magog in Revelation 20:7 - 9, is post Millennial." There seems much evidence for two great battles to conclude *"the end of days"*, separated by the 1000 year reign of Christ on the present earth.

The exact timing of this first great "Gog" conflict, most likely at the Second Coming of Jesus, (Rev 19:11-21) will be revealed as current events in the Middle East regarding the security of Israel unfold. It will occur when Israel is living in expected *"security"*. At this time (2010) their existence as a nation is under constant threat, and they are being pressured to give up land and Jerusalem. See Luke 21:24.

Chapters 40 - 48   Detail of a new temple to be built as a *"place of My throne and the place for the soles of My feet. This is where I will live among the Israelites forever..."*. The *"glory of the Lord"* returns to the temple (43:6, 7). Also detailed are the temple services and divisions of the land among the twelve tribes. All of this is shown to Ezekiel in an extensive vision as the prophet is carried back to the land of Israel, shown the new temple, the new order of service and the division of the land among the tribes when they shall have returned. Jehovah had promised in the latter part of Chapter 37 that He would dwell with them as their God forever.

Ezekiel

Whether the vision in these chapters is to be considered to be fulfilled literally, or in a figurative or symbolic way, commentators differ widely from one another. The figurative interpretation was the predominate one from the earliest of Church history, but in more recent times many of the most learned scholars have not hesitated to champion the literal explanation for this prophesy. This is especially true now that Israel occupies much of the land and is planning to build a new temple in Jerusalem. (See Matthew 24:16) The current temple plans are not the same plans as laid out in these chapters of Ezekiel. The Ezekiel temple may be the Millennium temple.

Ezekiel sees in the vision the temple as a finished building, with much detail. How all this fits in with *"the end of days"* is yet to be determined. (Rev Chapters 21 - 22)

Daniel　　　Written by the Prophet Daniel.　　　607 BC - 534 BC

Chapter 1　　　Daniel is introduced. He was an Israelite brought to Babylon after the fall of Jerusalem. He must have been a young man of noble birth and keen intellect (1:3, 4). God gave him *"knowledge and understanding of all kinds...and he could understand visions and dreams of all kinds".* (1:17)

2:31-45　　　The dream of a great image by Nebuchadnezzar, and it's interpretation rendered by Daniel. The head of gold was the Babylonian Empire (606 BC - 538 BC). The silver breast and arms represent the Medo-Persian Empire (538 BC - 371 BC). The brass belly and thighs the Grecian Empire (371 BC - 167 BC). These empires are quite universally acknowledged as historically correct.

The fourth kingdom is, by most serious studies, the Roman Empire. The historical evidence argues strongly for this view. This fourth kingdom corresponds to the fourth beast in Chapter 7, and the division of the Roman Empire into Eastern and Western Kingdoms. Also, the exposition of the *"seventy weeks"* in Chapter 9 favors the fulfillment of the various prophecies to Rome.

The Roman Empire began in 167 BC with it's conquering of the four divisions of the Grecian Empire, and ended as a world empire in 476 AD. The *"legs of iron"* in verse 33 represent, no doubt, the split into the Eastern and Western Kingdoms. At some time in the future a ten kingdom confederacy will emerge as a revived Roman Empire, as represented by the *"ten toes"* of the image (verse 44). Ten toes could relate to five (kings) nations from both east and west.

The *"stone cut out of the mountain"* in verse 45 is the Kingdom of Christ. In Matthew 21:44 and Luke 20:18 Jesus clearly refers this Messianic prophecy to Himself and His Kingdom.

7:1-28   Daniel's dream/vision of the four beasts and it's interpretation refers to the same things as Nebuchadnezzar's vision in Chapter 2. The fourth beast (Roman Empire) is the focus, and the ten kings to arise are generally believed to be identical with the beast in Revelation 13. Revelation 17:12 says the kings *"have as yet received no kingdom"*, and therefore the reference here cannot be to any kingdom before the date of writing of the Book of Revelation (96 AD). If this be so, the ten kingdom revived Roman Empire will be constructed just prior to the Great Tribulation.

A question arises; which Roman Kingdom, Eastern or Western, or both, will it come out of as a ten nation confederacy lead by the Antichrist? There are five toes on each side, perhaps representing both sides of the new kingdom, Eastern and Western.

Verse 8 describes *"another horn, a little one"*, that is typically considered to be the Antichrist of the New Testament (2 Thess 2:3-4, and others). The interpretation given in verse 21 says, *"the same horn made war with the saints, and prevailed against them"*.

Verse 25 continues with the blasphemy against God that is assumed by this individual, and to *"wear out the saints"*, and *"to change the times and the law"* (see below). Also stated is that, *"they (saints) shall be given into his hand (Antichrist) for three and one half years"*. Most commentators accept the only satisfactory explanation is a literal one, most likely the last half of the Great Tribulation.

About *"change the times"* Daniel 7:25:

Daniel

The Royal Mecca Clock Tower

In August, 2010, Greenwich Mean Time is being challenged as the world's source of standard time measurement. Muslims worldwide are expected to use this new clock in Mecca, Saudi Arabia, for setting their watches.

This world's largest timepiece is now ticking as part of the Royal Mecca Clock Tower which dominates Islam's holiest city. It is in the heart of a large complex funded by the Saudi government which includes hotels, shopping sites and conference halls. It will stand over Mecca's Grand Mosque. This new clock and tower has a close resemblance to the tower that houses Big Ben in London, England, and is huge in size.

The clock's four faces are over 150 feet in diameter and are illuminated by two million LED lights. The clock will show "Arabia Standard Time", which is three hours ahead of GMT. In addition to the huge clock faces there is large Arabic script that reads, "In the name of Allah".

Standing nearly 2000 feet tall, it is currently the world's second tallest building, and can be seen from many miles away. It will also remind the residents of Mecca of the time to pray five times a day.

Islamic scholars expect the clock's influence will fulfill their plans for it to replace the Greenwich Observatory as the "true center of the earth". It will become the standard time by which all other timepieces on earth will be set. "Putting Mecca time in the face of Greenwich Mean Time... this is the goal."

Further claims include that the GMT is centered on the old world of "colonialism", and that Mecca is the center of the world and provides a better location due to its "zero magnetism zone". This is disputed by Western scientists.

GMT has been the center of standard time for over 125 years.

- Gleaned from various news sources

About *"change the law"*, Daniel 7:25:

It is well known that Islam desires to control the "law" (Shari'ah)wherever it is established. Their version of "law" requires all to adhere to Islam teachings and to become a Moslem. All other religions are considered "infidels", especially "the people of the Book, Jews and Christians". "Infidels" are beheaded, or otherwise killed. (Revelation 20:4)

7:13,14   These verses give a preview of the Second Coming of the *"Son of Man"*. Jesus persistently called Himself the Son of Man. Fausset calls attention to the fact that it is a title always associated with the Second Coming of Christ. He comes *"with the clouds of heaven"* in judgment (Rev 19:11-16). In verse 18 is seen the *"saints of the Most High shall receive the kingdom and possess the kingdom forever"*.

7:18   Who are these saints? These are not the angels of verses 10 and 16, but they are the people of God. But, what people of God? Here is a controversy as yet not fully resolved. There are three primary views given:

1. The glorified saints. But, this cannot be, for verses 21 and 25 say the *"little horn makes war on them and wears them out."* They must therefore be God's people on earth at that time (a period of three and one half years during the Great Tribulation).

2. The people of Christ - the faithful Church. If it is found that the Church is to pass through the Tribulation period, or a portion of it, this explanation is quite plausible, and probably the correct one. (2 Thess 2:1-8; Matt 24:29-31; Rev 6:9-11; Luke 18:7, 8; Rev 20:4)

3. Daniel's own people, the Israelites converted and God-fearing, the portion of them who are supposed to be on earth after the Church has been caught away. If the Church does not go through the Tribulation, or some part of it, then this explanation is without doubt the correct one. (Rev 7:1-8)

7:28   Concludes, *"Here is the end of the matter..."*. This refers to the whole vision and as noted in verses 26-27, the *"judgment is set"*, and the *"greatness of the kingdoms under the whole heaven shall be given to the people of the saints of the Most High..."*. (Rev 20:4-6, 21:1-8)

8:1-26   Daniel's vision of the ram and goat, and it's interpretation by the angel, Gabriel. In verses 3-14 Daniel is found giving specific details about a *"ram with two horns: and a "he-goat coming from the West"*. The goat from the West defeats the ram. There is much speculation regarding the identity of these represented kingdoms, and the time of their occurrence.

Daniel

Scofield says, "The little horn here is a prophecy fulfilled in Antiochus Epiphanes in 175 BC, and is not to be confused with the little horn of Chapter 7, who is yet to come and will dominate the earth in the Great Tribulation." He also says, referring to verses 10-14, "This passage is confessedly the most difficult in prophecy, a difficulty increased by the state of the text."

In verses 15-26 is the interpretation of the vision given to Daniel by the angel Gabriel (verse 16), who said, *"the vision concerns the time of the end"*. Gabriel states in verse 19, *"I am going to tell you what will happen later in the time of wrath, because the vision concerns the appointed time of the end"*. (Rev 11:18, 14:9-12)

Scofield, and others, have difficulty with the *"appointed time of the end"*. Scofield thinks, "Two ends are in view here". This seems to contradict the plain explicit words of the angel, Gabriel. In any case, Daniel is told in verse 25 *"to seal up the vision, for it concerns the distant future"*.

9:2-9   Daniel's prayer, confession and request to the Lord. Daniel studied the *"Scriptures according to the word of the Lord given to Jeremiah, that the desolation of Jerusalem would last seventy years"*.

That period of time was almost at it's close in 538 BC, when the prayer and vision occurred. Daniel studied and accepted this prophecy in Jeremiah as literal and expected.

9:20-27   The vision, *"Seventy weeks"* and it's interpretation given by angel Gabriel. This is the foundational reference to God's process and timing to redeem His people, and the earth.

9:24   *"Seventy weeks are decreed upon thy people..."* -

It is conceded by all that these are weeks of years; more accurately "sevens of years", which equals 490 years. Four hundred and ninety years are to elapse before the everlasting righteousness is established. There are six specific events, or occurrences, mentioned that complete this process of God's dealing with humanity in it's present condition:

1. *"to finish transgression"*, to complete, restrain, hem in, hinder it, so that transgression can no longer spread.

2. *"to make an end of sins"*, literally to seal up, to conceal, to remove from God's sight, so as to never be declared against God's chosen people. (Psalm 103:9-12)

3. *"reconciliation for iniquity"* means to atone for by sacrifice, as meaning the doctrine of reconciliation belonging to the New Testament. (Rom 3:25, 5:8, 9)

4. *"everlasting righteousness"* as imputed to the Believer by the righteousness of Christ and practiced by the faithful Believer. (Rom 1:16, 17)

5. *"to seal up vision and prophecy"*, in the sense of causing it to cease due to its fulfillment.

6. *"to anoint the most holy"*, is the completion of the process and the culmination of God's dealing with mankind's rebellion by the establishment of the dwelling place of God on earth. (Rev Chapters 21, 22)

9:25   *"From the going forth of the commandment"* - the timing of the vision is set. There are four commands, or decrees issued that one of which seems the *"seventy weeks"* ought to be dated. They are:

1. Decree of Cyrus in 536 BC (Ezk 6:14; Isa 44:28)

2. Decree of Darius in 519 BC that continued the Cyrus decree (Ezk 6:12)

3. Decree of Artaxerxes Longimanus in 457 BC (Ezk 7:1, 8:11)

4. Artaxerxes second decree in 445 BC (Neh 2:1, 7). In addition to these there are advocates of other starting points for the 490 years.

A prophetic year is usually considered to be 360 days by most scholars.

"Seven weeks, and three score and two weeks" - sixty-nine weeks, or 483 years, are declared for the accomplishment of the *"rebuilding of Jerusalem"* for *"the anointed one, the prince"*, after which *"the anointed one be cut off...the city and sanctuary to be destroyed"*. Jerusalem and the temple were destroyed by the Romans in 70 AD. Most all commentators consider *"the anointed one"* to be Jesus Christ. Daniels vision proved to be accurate and literally fulfilled.

9:26   *"After the 62 weeks the Anointed One will be cut off and will have nothing."* Scofield says, "The crucifixion is the first event of verse

Daniel

26. The second event is the destruction of the city fulfilled in 70 AD. Then *'war will continue until the end'* is a period not fixed, but which has already lasted almost 2000 years. To Daniel it was only revealed that wars and desolations should continue (Matt 24:6-14). The New Testament reveals that which was hidden from the Old Testament prophets (Eph 3:1-10). During this unspecified period of time should be accomplished the mysteries of the Kingdom of Heaven (Matt 13:1-15). When the Church Age will end and the 'seventieth week' begin is nowhere revealed. It's duration can be but seven years; to make it more violates the principle of interpretation already confirmed by fulfillment."

9:27 Most modern commentators believe the activities and events of this verse refer to Antichrist - "that ungodly prince shall impose upon the mass of people a strong covenant that they should follow him and give themselves to him as their god" - Keil. Scofield says, "He will covenant with the Jews to restore their temple sacrifices...he will break the covenant and fulfill Daniel 12:11; 2 Thessalonians 2:3 ,4." (Matt 24:15-28; Dan 12:1; Rev 3:10)

10:14 Daniel has a vision of *"a man"*. This *"man"* is a messenger from God and announces a prophecy for the end times. He comes *"to explain to you what will happen to your people in the future...a time yet to come"*. The vision is given in the following chapter.

Chapter 11 Daniel first traces through a prophetic vision the history of the Grecian Empire which had to do with Palestine and the Jews, Syria and Egypt. This vision of kings and kingdoms, wars and destructions, leads up to the time of Antiochus Epiphanes in verse 21. Some may also acquaint this to the activities of Antichrist at a future time as well.

11:31-35 Here is the *"little horn"* of Chapter 8, Antiochus Epiphanes, in Palestine. This is the time when he *"profaned the sanctuary...set up the abomination"*, and pollutes the temple by setting up an altar to the god Jupiter Olympius, sacrifices a sow and sprinkles it about the temple. Scofield says of verse 35, "Daniel overleaps the centuries to the time of the Antichrist of the final end time...when God's wrath is completed." (Rev 14:9-12, 11:36-39)

11:36-39 The willful king is described. It seems to identify the characteristics of the coming Antichrist, of which Antiochus Epiphanes was a type. This persons arrogance and self esteem is paramount, as *"he shall exalt himself, and magnify himself above every god...he shows no respect for any god, and has no desire of women".* (2 Thess 2:4) This cannot be a description of Antiochus Epiphanes, since he recognized and sacrificed to the god Jupiter.

11:40-45   The martial career of the willful king is somewhat difficult to know to whom these verses apply. Some views relate the verses to expeditions by Antiochus Epiphanes, however ancient historical writings know nothing about such an expedition as described here. Those who refer verses 36-39 to the final Antichrist refer these verses to him also. (Rev 13)

Chapter 12   Tells of tribulation and resurrection. Probably a transition was made at 11:35 from the events relating to Antiochus Epiphanes, to the final Antichrist. Most expositors find in these verses the final time of the Great Tribulation and the Second Coming of Christ.

12:1-4   Michael, the protecting archangel of the Jewish people, *"will arise at that time".* (1 Thess 4:16; 2 Thess 2:7; Rev 12:7) *"There will be a time of distress such as has not happened...",* then a physical resurrection takes place. There is debate about to which resurrection this refers; the general resurrection at the end of all things (Rev 20:11-15), or to a partial resurrection immediately after the Great Tribulation, that is confined to Daniel's own nation; *"but, at that time your people - everyone whose name is found written in the book - will be delivered."*

Fausset says, "The same deliverance of Israel as in Zechariah 13:8, 9, ...the remnant spared according to the observation of the Lord Jesus Christ when they shall see Him at His Second Coming, and the Spirit of grace and supplication is poured out on them."
(Zech 12:10, 11, 13:1; Rom 11:25-27)

The Jews do not seem to be converted back to God in large numbers until the Great Tribulation period and their experience with the Antichrist. Perhaps there are Jewish witnesses to proclaim the Gospel to the unconverted Jews during that time?
(Rev 11:3-12, 14:1-5)

Another idea concerns the resurrection at the rapture of the faithful Church, which in context with these verses would occur toward the end of, or at the end of, the Great Tribulation period.
(Matt 24:29-31, 25:31-46; 1 Thess 4:16, 17; 1 Cor 15:20-26; Rev 20:4-6)

Daniel

In verse 4 Daniel is instructed to *"close up and seal the words of the scroll until the time of the end"*. This refers to the whole book, and it will be better studied and understood later. The *"many shall run to and fro"* is better said as in the NIV, *"many will go here and there to increase knowledge"*, in the sense of searching, scrutinizing, investigating the prophecy to gain understanding to increase knowledge. The idea of "travel for a purpose" is included.

12:5-9   Daniel's prophetic vision now includes two angels who provide more information about the events foretold. *"How long shall it be to the end of these wonders?"* A three and one half year period is again told of, but its full meaning is *"sealed until the time of the end...the wise will understand"*.

12:10-13   Daniel's desire for knowing more is deferred to *"the time of the end"*. Fausset says, "John's Revelation in part reveals what here is veiled...when the predictions so far given shall have come to pass, the godly shall be purified by the foretold trials and shall understand that the end is at hand; but, the wicked shall not understand..."
(Jer 23:20; Hosea 3:4, 5; Matt 24:32-35; 1 Thess 5:4)

A further explanation of the three and one-half year period is given as a 1290 day period beginning with the taking away of the daily sacrifice and the setting up of the *"abomination that makes desolate"*. No doubt this is referred to the time of Antichrist. There are several varied explanations, each marking the fall of Antichrist as 1290 days from the *"abomination"*. The additional 45 days mentioned (1335 days) probably marks the beginning of the Millennium.

The angels conclude with instruction and encouragement to Daniel. He was to go on to the end of his life, and rest in the grave and was to rise again to enjoy his share of the promised inheritance.

According to Wycliffe; *"'rest in the grave'*, finds his spirit rejoicing in the presence of God, where he would *'see His face'*. (Rev 22:4; Luke 16:19-22) Philippians 1:23 says, *'to depart, and to be with Christ in Paradise'* (Luke 23:43). It is a time of rest, as we read here, in the bosom of Abraham (Luke 16:22) and a time of comfort (Luke 16:25). There is a *'crown of righteousness'* laid up which our Lord will give us in that day.

On this calm note of rest and immeasurable joy, the book of Daniel comes to a close. Daniel faithfully fulfilled his purpose, and would be so rewarded."

Hosea   Written by the Prophet Hosea.   785 BC - 725 BC

1:1   The Word of the Lord came to Hosea about 150 years before Daniel, and his time in captivity in Babylon. Israel and Judah had not yet been captured by Nebuchadnezzar.

1:10, 11   The future blessing and restoration of Israel is prophesied by the Lord to Hosea. A complete and literal fulfillment of the restoration of the Jews is still to come. Verse 10 most likely refers to the ten tribes of Israel, and their great numbers as they are dispersed throughout the earth. Verse 11 brings both Israel and Judah *"gathered together, and they shall appoint themselves one head...".* There is some debate about the meaning, but it is clear the Apostle Paul understood this prophecy as pointing to a spiritual fulfillment, proven by Romans 9:22-26. The complete and final literal fulfillment is yet in view.

2:14-23   The promise of Israel's conversion and renewal of the covenant. In the preceding verses the punishment of Israel for her sins has caused her to long for God. *"In that day...you will call Me 'my husband'"* (verse 6), is the Lord's declaration that Israel will recognize Jehovah as her true spouse, and will have rejected all other *"gods".* The literal fulfillment of this in the promised land must be a part of the final restoration in the end times.

3:4, 5   The future kingdom, the Messianic days and the reestablishment of the Jewish nation will yet return and seek Jehovah their God.

Chapters 4 - 10 Mostly contain the Lord's charges and punishments against Israel.

11:8-11   Jehovah's longing and purpose to restore Israel, and His intention to bring them back from their dispersion. His desire is *"not to give them up...to not come in wrath"*, but to subdue their enemies and cause them, *"to dwell in their houses".* The fulfillment of this, of course, is to

Hosea

happen at *"the end"*. Now that the nation of Israel *"dwells in their houses"*, the final time of fulfillment must be near. (Hosea 12:9; Zech 14:4-8)

13:14   The promise here is to *"ransom them from the power of sheol; I will redeem them from death..."*. The literal fulfillment in the establishment of the new nation of Israel in these days prepares the way for this promise to be fulfilled for the Jewish people. Jesus victory over death and the grave, His resurrection and soon coming again will bring about the full harvest in the resurrection at the end. (Dan 12:1-4; 1 Cor 15:55, 56)

14:4-7   The Lord's love and healing of Israel; His blessings in a future time will be poured out. The restoration, redemption and blessing of the Lord on His people and their land will be accomplished in His perfect time. *"The ways of the Lord are right..."* (14:9).

Joel   Written by the Prophet Joel.   800 BC

1:4,6,15   The beginning of the Day of Jehovah is a description of a plague and an invasion of a hostile army. Is this an allegorical prediction, or a literal calamity? A good case can be made for either; but in either case it is a portent of a coming calamity, as *"the day of Jehovah"* is always a day of judgment, a day of His anger. The prophet predicts famine and drought and a call for prayer and fasting.

2:1-11   An invading army from the North (verse 20) of unrivaled might appears to come into the nation, compared to swarms of locusts in Chapter 1. Scofield takes this prophecy of being that which is described in Revelation 19:11-18, the battle foretold being the battle of Armageddon. (Rev 9:1-12)

2:12-17   A call to repentance is declared by the Lord to the people of Zion. A plea by the priests who minister in the temple, *"Spare your people, O' Lord..."*. If this calamity does refer to the end times, then temple worship in the nation of Israel is being conducted.

2:18-27   The Lord answers with a promise of final deliverance, *"never again will I make you an object of scorn to the nations"* (verse 19). In verse 20 *"the northern army"* most likely refers to the Gentile world powers headed up by the Beast and the False Prophet (Rev 16:12 -14). The final verses here promise an abundance of food and blessings as," *Never again will My people be shamed"* (Isa 45:17).

2:28-32   The Day of the Lord is described here as one of promise and an outpouring of the Spirit, as well as judgment. The beginning of the fulfillment of this prophecy is related to Acts 2:17. It has a partial and continuous fulfillment in these *"last days"*, which began with the First Advent of Christ. Many people will *"prophesy...dream dreams...see visions"*, as God *"pours out His Spirit in those days"*. These are the three modes whereby God revealed Himself to humanity in the Old Testament. He has further revealed Himself through His Son, Jesus, in the New Testament, as well as through prophecy, dreams and visions. The Holy Spirit has been given in these *"last days"* to multitudes of Believers, and His outpouring is a sign of the very end of days.

Verses 30 - 32 describe the cosmical signs preceding the day of the Lord. There must be terrible convulsions of nature before the final destruction of the ungodly world. (Matt 24:21-31) During this *"great and dreadful day of the Lord"*, a wonderful promise is made; *"everyone who calls on the Lord will be saved..."*. Does this refer to the Jewish people in Israel only? In the days of the Destruction of Jerusalem in 70 AD, the Christians were saved by heeding Jesus words in Matthew 24:16 and Luke 21:20, by leaving Jerusalem and retiring to Pella. The Lord provides deliverance to *"whom the Lord calls"*, according to the election of grace (Rom 11:5). Most expositors are in agreement here.

3:1-8   The restoration of Israel and the judgment of her enemies *"in those days"*. These are the days when the Jews are brought back from captivity and living on part of the promised land, as they now do today. Judgment is pronounced on *"all nations"*, who are primarily those that have offended against Israel, but also inclusive of the heathen world in general. God will cause them to gather *"down in the valley of Jehosaphat"*, where He will *"execute judgment upon them"*. These nations have wronged the people of Israel, *"for they scattered My people among the nations and divided up My land"*. Today Israel is a *"parted land"* that is under threat of further division to appease world powers. Reference Luke 21:24. (Ezekiel Chapters 38 - 39)

3:9-16   The nations are here summoned to come against Israel. Their madness towards God's people shall cause the nation's to move from

Joel

peaceful efforts to preparation for war. Their motive is to destroy Israel completely, but instead they will be destroyed. Verses 12-16 portray the vengeance of the Lord on His enemies. It is a gruesome and horrific scene. (Ezk 38:18-23; Jer 25:30-31; Isa 63:4-6, 66:15, 16)

3:17-21 The foregoing events prepare for the blessings of the coming kingdom. God's people will *"then know that I, the Lord your God, will dwell in Jerusalem...as it will be holy"*. Jerusalem will never again be invaded. Israel will be a place of peaceful abundance, and the dwelling place of the Lord.
(Joel 2:30-32; Matt 25:31-34; Rev 21)

Amos Written by the Prophet Amos. 787 BC - 763 BC

Amos, *"one of the shepherds of Tekoa"*, called by God to prophesy in the Northern Kingdom of Israel, to warn and proclaim judgment on Israel for her sins and rebellion. Within fifty years his warnings were fulfilled, the kingdom being utterly destroyed, and the people dispersed. The visions of Amos included the destruction of surrounding nations and certain aspects to the *"whole house of Jacob"*.

The future judgment on Judah was fulfilled in the seventy years captivity in Babylon, and the judgment on Israel, the Northern Kingdom, in the world wide dispersion which continues to this day, even though many Jews from the countries of the world are now returning to the reestablished nation of Israel.

3:2 The Jewish peoples were chosen as a special people, whose purpose was to honor God, the Deliverer, and to fulfill His covenants with Abraham, Isaac, Jacob, David, etc. Their many rebellions culminated in this judgment; *"therefore, I will punish you for all your sins."*

3:7 As a witness is summoned to provide true information for a just verdict in a trial, so *"the Sovereign Lord does nothing without revealing His plan to His servants the prophets"*. Prophets have historically called out the sins of the people, and given plenty of warning to encourage repentance. They are seldom respected and heard.

5:16-20   Amos reveals the reasons for the coming judgment and calls the nation to repent, to *"seek God, not evil, that you may live..."* (verse 14). God's righteous retribution and *"the Day of Jehovah"* are a terrible judgment, as there will be mourning for many dead, both in the cities and the countryside. Verse 18 provides a sobering warning to those who *"desire the Day of the Lord"*, for it will be a day of calamity and a day of righteous retribution, and not a day of victory. A day of no escape (9:1). This occurred because the people did not heed, nor obey the exhortations to repent (8:1-3). This is also a stern warning to future desires for the "Day of the Lord".

9:1; 8-10   A vision of Jehovah executing judgment on the ten tribes of Israel. The judgment is final and complete, as *"none shall escape"*, and God declares, *"I will destroy it (Israel) from off the face of the earth"*. To this day the whereabouts of the ten tribes of Israel are unknown. Even so, in verse 9 the Lord declares, *"yet I will not totally destroy the house of Jacob"*. A remnant of Judah would later, after the Babylonian captivity, reestablish the nation and temple worship to the time of the Messiah. This was, of course, accomplished after their captivity.

9:11-15   The blessings of the future kingdom arise out of the *"tabernacle of David that is fallen"*. This foretells not only the restoration after the Babylonian captivity, but looks to the restoration under Messiah. The promises in these verses are to be fulfilled when the Jews shall have been restored to their own land. This is now in process, and in spite of the clatter of their enemies, *"they shall no more be plucked up out of their land I have given them, says the Lord your God"*.

Obadiah   Writer unknown, obscure.   586 BC (?)

In this short book the writer is not identified. He, no doubt, is recording a message from the Lord about the *"Day of Jehovah"* and the punishment of the ungodly in verses 1-16. The *"people of Esau"* are condemned *"because of the violence against your brother Jacob, you will be covered with shame, you will be destroyed forever"*. The *"people of Esau"* still exist today as some of the Turks, Palestinians and other Arabs, according to some studies.

In verses 15-16 is seen a universal judgment *"upon all nations"*. (Joel 3:14; Zech 12:3)

Obadiah

In verses 17-21 is found the reestablishment of the Jews *"in their possessions"*. The *"house of Jacob"* is the kingdom of Judah, and the *"house of Joseph"* is the kingdom of Israel. Together they shall form one kingdom of *"fire and flame that shall consume"* the *"house of Esau for stubble"*. Fausset says, "This was but an earnest of the future union of Judah and Israel in the possession of the enlarged land as one kingdom." He was correct, as this "possession" is now in process. (Ezk 37:15-17) It seems the *"people of Esau"* will join with Antichrist and be destroyed in the *"Day of Jehovah"*. (Gen 27:40) Also refer to Ezekiel Chapters 38 and 39.

Biederwolf states emphatically, "In as much as the distribution of the land as set forth in these verses has never taken place, it would seem as though it ought to take place in the future...to be fully accomplished with its final completion at the Second Coming of the Lord." His literal interpretation of these verses seems to be proven correct.

| **Micah** | Written by the Prophet Micah. | 750 BC - 710 BC |

2:12,13   God's promise to the remnant of Judah and Israel to put them back together and make them a *"multitude of men"*. The restoration from Babylon was partial. The literal fulfillment is still to come, as mentioned in Romans 11:25-27.

4:1-13   The future kingdom and the regathering of Israel *"in the latter days shall come to pass"*. The first three verses are almost word for word like Isaiah 2:2-4. Isaiah probably quoted from Micah. In verse 3 is found a promise that the nations *"shall learn war no more"*. This occurs at the end of the Millennium. (Rev 20:7-10)

The Lord reveals His plan for the future kingdom in the Millennium, after the suffering of the Jewish people in the Babylonian captivity (verse 10) that cured them of idol worship, and the final dispersion after the destruction of Jerusalem and the nation in 70 AD. This final time of suffering and rejection must cure them of their unbelief.

The remnant will be made into a strong nation in the latter years (verse 7). The generation living from 1948 until the present is most likely witnessing this prophecy being fulfilled.

5:1-15   A major prophecy about Jesus the Messiah, the dispersion of Israel, and the Kingdom Age. In verse 2 is announced the birth place of a coming *"ruler of Israel, whose goings forth are from old, from everlasting"*. No doubt a reference to Jesus birth, and origin. (Luke 1:32, 33; John 1:1; Matt 2:1) Verses 3-5 provide an overview of the history of the Jewish people and the nation of Israel until their final redemption; *"and He will be their peace"*.

Verses 5-15 show the peoples future dispersion; *"the remnant of Jacob will be in the midst of many peoples...will be among the nations..."*. Finally, Israel will become *"as a lion, a nation of power that through it and by it God may smite His enemies"* (verse 15).

7:1-6   A description of a wicked world, a world of ungodly people; *"their hands are upon that which is evil to do it diligently..."*. This describes conditions in the last days; *"the day of thy watchman, even thy visitation is come; now shall be their perplexity."* This foretells conditions in the day of the Lord and His righteous judgment.

7:7-20   Israel's distress in the end time will cause her *"to look unto Jehovah"*. Henry Alford says, "As she did under Babylonian captivity and so shall she do again when the Spirit of Grace shall be poured out upon her." The *"rebuilding"* foretold in verse 11 anticipates the ending of the Babylonian exile and restoration of the people to the land of Israel, but the final restoration of the nation is seen also.

Verse 13 predicts calamity on the earth because of the evil deeds of its inhabitants. This prophecy continues as *"nations...turn in fear to the Lord our God, and will be afraid of you."* Finally, is seen the grace and forgiveness of God towards *"the remnant of His Inheritance"*. (Psalm 103; Isa 57:16; Rom 11:5)

Zephaniah   Written by the Prophet Zephaniah.   630 BC - 611 BC

Chapter one contains warning and consequence when Jehovah's day of wrath comes upon the earth. The first judgments here are against the Jewish people by the Chaldeans (verse 7). Also the references in verses 14-19 describe the final judgments on humanity; *"in the fire of His jealousy the whole world will be consumed, for He will make an end of all who live on the earth."* (Rev 21:1)

Zephaniah

2:1-11 Here continues the judgment against Judah due to their pride and insolent attitude. A plea for repentance and a possibility of being *"hid in the day of Jehovah's anger"*. The remnant of Judah, upon her return from exile is to inherit the land as pasture for her flocks. Included here is the final promise of restoration to the land so that, *"the nations on every shore will worship Him, everyone in his own land"*.

3:1-7 In these verses Jerusalem is denounced for the peoples rebellion and arrogance.

3:8-20 The future of Jerusalem's reestablishment promised. The assembly of nations to come against Jerusalem and the Jewish remnant is declared for God's last act of judgment. Kleinert says, "It is a fixed element of prophetic eschatology, the final gathering of the heathen nations before Jerusalem in order to be destroyed in the decisive struggle."
(Micah 4:12; Joel 3:2; Zech 12:2, 3, 14:2-4; Rev Chapters 19 and 20)

After the final judgment joyful righteousness is proclaimed for Israel in verses 14-20. (Psalm 46:8-11)

Haggai Probably written by a Prophet so named. 520 BC

2:6-9 The glory of the future temple which shall be greater than that of Solomon's. This temple is one *"in yet a little while"*, and God's judgments are represented as, *"I will shake the heavens...shake the nations"*. I will judge (Psa 110:6) until they shall lose hostility to God. Fausset says, "This denotes the beginning of the end of the latter days...the shaking began introductory to the First Advent; it will be finished at the Second. Concerning the First Advent: Matt 3:17, 27:51, 28:2; Acts 2:2, 4:31. Concerning the latter compare Matt 24:7; Rev 16:17-20, 18:20, 20:11."

Sir Isaac Newton says here, "There is scarcely a prophecy of the Messiah in the Old Testament which does not to some extent at least refer to His Second Coming."

This remarkable prediction about the *"glory"* of this temple has several possible meanings. God determines to *"fill this house with glory"*. He claims possession of *"the precious things of all nations...the silver and gold is mine"*. Materials are made available for a glorious structure. (Rev 21:11) The first temple was filled with the *"cloud of glory"*. This temple is to be filled with the glory of God veiled in the flesh (John 1:14), and the glory of Christ (Rev 21:23), according to Fausset.

What now as to the fulfillment of this remarkable prediction? *"This latter house"* can only refer to the temple yet to be built as predicted in Ezekiel Chapter 43. Is the temple currently being planned and prepared for construction in the new nation of Israel this temple? (This is likely the temple to be desolated by the Antichrist.) Probably not, but only in due time will we know.

This Ezekiel temple may be the Millennial temple before the *"new heaven and the new earth"* are established. (Zech 2:1-13; Rev 20:6)

2:20-23   The future destruction of the nations comes as a *"word of Jehovah the second time"*. Great convulsions of nature will accompany the events of *"that day"*, a period of time, however long, when the heathen nations are doubtless stirred up against each other and the wars will be mutually destructive; *"by the sword of his brother"*. (This is happening today with the ethnic wars and genocide occurring in various places.) "All other kingdoms", says Fausset, "are to be overthrown to make way for Christ's universal kingdom (Dan 2:44)."

"I will make thee as a signet" is somewhat a puzzling prediction. It is to occur *"in that day"* while the preceding judgments and wars are occurring. Zerubbabel, as the representative of his people, was a type of "seal", an object of constant regard.

Fausset says, "The theocratic people, and their representative, Zerubbabel, the type, and Messiah his descendent the antitype, are regarded by God (Rom 11:25-29)."

It seems that during the commotions God would take care of Zerubbabel, as representative of the people, during the construction of the temple. This assurance of safety at this time no doubt refers to *"in that day"*, and also to the time of the reconstructions in Jerusalem after the Babylonian captivity.

The literal and final fulfillment of these prophecies now seems to be in process, as the nations of the world more openly condemn the Jewish

Haggai

people and Israel, and the "Christian" way of belief. Man's rebellion and apostasy toward his Creator is nearing completion as he works to control all aspects of the worlds governments, economies and religions to his own making. Refer to Addendum about the United Nations.

Zechariah   Written by the Prophet Zechariah.   520 BC - 487 BC

1:7-17   The rider on the red horse is the first of ten visions in one night. The red horse represents bloodshed, and implies vengeance on the foes of Israel. The other horses mentioned may represent burning and destroying, with the white horse perhaps a symbol of victory. The man on the red horse is either an angel, or Christ. The *"seventy years"* and *"a line stretched forth over Jerusalem"* represents a measuring line for extending the city. The contents of this were all practically fulfilled under Ezra and Nehemiah, but this was only a beginning.

1:18, 19   The vision of the *"four horns"*. A horn is usually the symbol of power, and here probably stands for a Gentile foe. The *"four horns"* most likely refers to the four cardinal points of the compass, as Israel had threatening foes on every side. This is still seen today, as the new nation of Israel struggles to survive while being surrounded by nations committed to their destruction.

Also to be considered by many is the four horns represent the four great world empires of Daniel.

1:20, 21   The vision of the four craftsmen represent various powers which God raised up to overthrow Israel's foes, and to *"cast down the horns of the nations"* mentioned in verses 18 and 19. If the four horns represent the four world empires of Daniel, then all have been overthrown. One, the Roman empire, or some aspect of it, will be resurrected in the end time (Dan 2:40-44).

2:1-13   The vision of *"a man with a measuring line in his hand"*. This chapter is a prophecy of the enlargement and security of the covenant people; of the restoration of the nation and Jerusalem. Scofield says, "The measuring line is used by Ezekiel (Ezk 40:3-5) as a symbol of preparation for rebuilding the city and the temple in the kingdom age." It seems a partial fulfillment is now in process in the new nation of Israel.

The Lord promises to regather His people *"from the four winds"*, and to restore the glory of His presence in Jerusalem and to execute judgment on the nations. In verses 10-13 is seen the full blessings of the earth in the kingdom age, when Jehovah *"will dwell in the midst of thee, and many nations shall join themselves to Jehovah in that day."* (Rev 21:24)

In the future God will not be confined to the Jews, but will be enlarged, as many Gentile peoples will be received through the Messianic age. (Zech Chapter 14)

3:1-7   In this vision of Joshua, the High Priest, he represents the people in his function as High Priest, performing his duties. Joshua's being *"clothed with filthy garments"* represents the sins of the people. Satan is the chief adversary, the accuser of the people and is to be finally rebuked by God through Messiah. Sins are forgiven by Jehovah; *"I have caused thine inequity to pass from thee...".* The divine forgiveness is dependent upon repentance and *"walking in My ways...keep My charge...".*

3:8-10   The vision of Jehovah's servant, the Branch, is the Messiah, Jesus, the chief cornerstone of the foundation of the Church. (Psalm 118:22) The stone that shall crush all the world kingdoms. (Matt 21:44)

4:1-14   The vision of the golden candlestick and the two olive trees. Scofield says, "This is, as we know from Revelations 11:3-12, a prophecy to be fulfilled in the last days of the present age." The candlestick symbolizes the Jewish theocracy and ultimately the Church. Fausset says, "The Gentile churches will not realize their unity until the Jewish church, as the stem, unites all the lamps in one candlestick (Rom 11:16-24)."

"The two anointed ones" (verse 14) at this point, probably refer to Joshua and Zerubbabel, who typify the royal and priestly office of Christ. Scofield says, "The whole scene forms a precursive fulfillment of the ministry of the two witnesses of Revelation Chapter 11, and the coming of the true headstone, Prince Messiah."

5:1-4   The vision of the flying scroll: the curse of God on the thief and the profane man.

Zechariah

5:5-11   The vision of the woman in a basket some think is a prophecy of the present dispersion of the Jewish people. Scofield thinks it relates to the Gentile church, in which the time of full iniquity falls under the severe judgment of God (Rev Chapter 18).

6:1-8   The vision of the four chariots sent forth to execute God's judgments on the wicked Gentile nations. It is a judgment going in every direction. *"Red"* denotes war and bloodshed; *"Black"* denotes sorrow and death; *"White"* denotes victory; and *"dappled"* denotes a mixed judgment of perhaps famine and pestilence. Scofield says, "That which is symbolized by the four chariots with their horses...is the four spirits of heaven which go forth from standing before the Lord...these spirits are angels, most naturally interpreted as the four angels of Revelation 7:1-3; 9:14, 15. The vision, then, speaks of the Lord's judgments upon the Gentile nations north and south in the Day of the Lord (Isa 2:10-22; Rev 19:11, 12)."

6:9-15   The crown for Joshua is to be made from the gold and silver sent as gifts for the temple from the exiles in Babylon. The Branch, Messiah, Priest and King, *"shall grow up out of His place"* as a genuine receiver of the promise made to build the temple of Jehovah. The spiritual temple is in thought, which is beyond the material temple they were building then.

8:1-8   Jehovah is determined to return and make His dwelling in Jerusalem, and promises future blessings on the people there. Verses 4-5 paint a beautiful scene of long life, security and happiness. The fulfillment is to be referred to Messianic times in the Millennium.

The scattered *"remnant"* is prophesied to return to Jerusalem from all lands, east and west, as far as the sun shines. The literal interpretation calls for an actual restoration to their own land, which is now in progress since 1948.

8:9-19   A call from Jehovah to heed the prophets, for they foretold of the rebuilding of the temple at that time. *"The seed of peace...you shall be a blessing"* is promised as an inheritance for the remnant. Fausset says, "The distinct mention of Judah and Israel proves that the prophecy has not yet had its full accomplishment, since Israel (the ten tribes) has never yet been restored, although individuals from Israel did return with Judah (from Babylon)."

8:20-23   Jerusalem is to be the religious center of the earth, as *"many peoples and strong nations shall come to seek Jehovah of hosts in Jerusalem..."*. (Zech Chapter 14)

9:1-8   A graphic account of Alexanders conquest in Syria, in the language of prophecy, and also a prophecy of Philistias incorporation with Judah. Scofield says, "The greater meaning of these verses converges on the yet future last days...".

9:9-17   The future coming of Zion's King is announced, as a prophecy fulfilled by Jesus, as he rode into Jerusalem for the Passover (Matt 21:1-5), just before His crucifixion. These verses look forward to the end time and the kingdom to be established in the promised land. The safety and peace to come is because of the coming Messiah whose dominion will be universal.

10:1-8   The Lord will care for a restored Judah and Israel. Deliverance is promised in verses 3-5, as God's blessings are poured out on the Jews in Palestine. Scofield says, "The whole scene is of events in the time of the northern invasion under the Beast (Dan 7:8 and Rev 19:20), and Armageddon (Rev 16:14, 19:17). The final deliverance is affected by the return of the Lord."

10:9-12   The dispersion and the regathering of Israel will be accomplished. Obstacles to their regathering will be removed by Jehovah and the people will *"walk up and down in His name"*.

11:7-14   The deliberate and persistent wickedness of Israel caused her rejection and punishment. "Her rejection of Messiah lead to the destruction of Jerusalem in 70 AD", says Scofield.

11:15-17   The judgment of the worthless or wicked shepherd. Who is meant here? Scofield says, "The reference to the Beast is obvious; no other personage of prophecy in any sense meets the description." Fausset says, "They were given up to Rome and shall be again given up to Antichrist, the instrument of judgment, by Christ's permission."

Chapters 12 - 14   Form one prophecy, the general theme of which is the Return of the Lord and the establishment of the Kingdom.

12:1-3   Here is prophesied that a day is coming when *"all the nations of the earth shall be gathered against it* (Jerusalem)". Jerusalem will

Zechariah

be the *"burdensome stone"* and center of the world's attention, causing the anti-Christian confederacy to come to their destruction at Armageddon. Today the critical attention on Jerusalem and Israel is a worldwide attention.

12:4-10   The siege against Israel and Jerusalem is described. Many commentators refer this prophecy to the dealings of God with national Israel in the last days. Verses 9-10 foretell the destruction of *"all the nations that attack Jerusalem"*, and the realization of the inhabitants of Jerusalem that their Savior is Messiah Jesus; *"and they will look on Me, the one they have pierced, and they will mourn for Him as one mourning for an only child ..."*. (John 3:16, John 19:36, 37; Rev 1:7)

12:11-14   The realization of Messiah Jesus will result in *"a great mourning in Jerusalem...and all the land shall mourn...all the families..."*. Grief pervades all the people from the highest rulers, the priestly line and to the lowest of families. There is a great repentance of the remnant. (Matt 24:30)

13:1-6   There will be a cleansing from sin, an end to idolatry and false prophesying. Idolatry as representing all forms of ungodliness and immorality; false prophesying as an active agency of deception in league with Satan, in direct contrast to the Spirit of Grace and Truth.

13:7-9   The shepherd struck, sheep scattered, the remnant refined and saved. This prophecy summarizes the rejection of Messiah, the scattering of the covenant peoples and their punishment. Keil says, "The dispersion of the flock will deliver two-thirds of the nation in the whole land to death, so that only one-third will remain alive (Ezk 5:2-12)." Literal death seems to be meant here, and this must await fulfillment in the future under Antichrist. Scofield contends this refers to the sufferings of the remnant preceding the great battle of Armageddon.

The Lord Comes and Reigns

14:1-3   *"A Day of Jehovah"* - A day appointed for the manifestation of His glory and power; the final conflict and triumph of God's Kingdom on earth. (Isa 24:1, 2)

14:4-8   The Second Coming of Messiah Jesus to the Mount of Olives, and the resulting physical changes in the land. The prediction that, *"His feet shall stand in that day upon the Mount of Olives"*, is a literal proof that the Lord is to return to this earth. (Acts 1:10, 11) He comes with *"all the holy ones"* (Rev 19:14). Most agree that angels are meant, but also could include glorified saints. This is a *"unique day"*, known only to Jehovah.

A great earthquake and cleavage of the land is predicted to occur at the time He stands on the Mount of Olives. A valley is created. Fausset says, "The valley reaches up to the city gates so as to enable the fleeing citizens (of Jerusalem) to immediately leave the city." One cannot imagine the panic, chaos and confusion of this scene. Verse 8 concludes an ever flowing stream towards the Dead Sea and toward the Mediterranean Sea; a lively image of abundance to come.

14:9-15   The Lord's Kingdom is established upon the earth; *"There shall be no more curse, Jerusalem shall dwell safely."* The *"last day"* will end everything, as those who have *"warred against Jerusalem"* will be utterly destroyed *"while they stand upon their feet"*. The horrible description of this destruction in verse 12 seems to depict what happens in a nuclear blast, but it may be a supernatural plague of Jehovah. The obvious foe that is punished is the Antichrist and his confederate nations (Rev 19:19-21).

14:16-21   After the great destruction of the anti-Christian confederacy, *"it shall come to pass that everyone that is left of all the nations that came against Jerusalem...shall worship the King, Jehovah of hosts...".* According to W. J. Erdman, "Here it is clearly taught that the Return of Christ is followed by the conversion of the world." This is a controversial view. If all the world is converted then why the release of Satan at the end of the Millennium, and the destruction of many peoples and nations (Rev 20:7-10)? Perhaps the conversion of the Jew is a more appropriate view. (Rom 11:12-15; 25-27; Isa 49:5-7; Acts 15:12-18; and others)

After the casting of Satan into the eternal lake of fire, then all the world is/has been converted, not immediately after the Return of Christ, as seems the thought by Erdman. See also the following comments by Fausset.

Fausset, referring the fulfillment of this prophecy to Millennium times, says, "That there shall be unconverted men during the time appears from the outbreak of Gog and Magog at the end of it (Rev 20:7-9), but they, like Satan their master, will be restrained during the Millennium."

Zechariah

"The representatives of these converted peoples and nations are called to Jerusalem for the yearly Feast of Tabernacles. Why is this feast designated? There are numerous reasons considered, but the best seems because of its historical relation as a feast of thanksgiving, after the Israelites pilgrimage through the desert. It was so kept on their return from Babylonian captivity. As they return to their land after the almost 2000 year dispersion, it will be again appropriate for the same season of thanksgiving.

Also, for the Gentiles it will be significant after their long wandering in their moral wilderness." - Biederwolf

Malachi   Written by the Prophet Malachi.   397 BC

Malachi was probably a Levite, and was chosen to be the final messenger of the prophetic word of the Old Testament. There is a 400 year prophetic gap until the New Testament begins.

2:17   The day of judgment is promised because the Lord *"is wearied...by (Judah) saying all who do evil are good in the eyes of the Lord"*. The unfaithfulness of Judah, and their lack of honor for the covenant relationship with God, has *"wearied"* Him.

Surely the Lord, today, is also "wearied" of mankind calling evil good, and good evil, as we see happening in our world at this present time. The sin and immorality of abortion, open sexual permissiveness, pornography of all sorts, the promotion of homosexuality as just another lifestyle, rampant corruption, disrespect for God and His people, etc., is an indictment that will no doubt soon bring the judgment of God upon the ungodly. Even so, presently there is still opportunity for repentance and revival before final judgment.

3:1-6   In response to Judah's sin, the Lord promised to send *"My messenger"*. These verses tell of the mission of John the Baptist and the coming of the Lord (Isa 40:3). The messenger is, of course, John the Baptist, who comes to *"prepare the way...for the Lord"*. It is evident that here Christ is meant, thus setting forth the deity of the Son of God, Jesus.

Scofield says, "Verses 2-5 speak of judgment, not grace. Malachi, in common with the other Old Testament prophets, saw both advents of the Messiah blended in one horizon, but did not see the separating interval of time described in Matthew Chapter 13, consequent upon rejection of the King (Matt 13:16-17). Still less was the Church Age in his vision. The *'messenger of the covenant'* is Christ in both of His Advents, but with special reference to the events which follow His Return (Matt 13:37-43)."

Fausset says, "His mission is here regarded as a whole from the First to Second Advent. The process of refining and separating the godly from the ungodly beginning during Christ's stay on earth, and going on ever since, is to continue until the final separation (Matthew 25:31-46). The refining process, whereby a third of the Jews is refined, as silver of it's dross, and a whole two-thirds perish is described (Zech 13:8, 9)."

3:16-18   The reward of the faithful remnant is *"a book of remembrance was written"* for their advantage against the day of judgment. They are to be *"mine own possession"*, literally *"mine own peculiar treasure"*. (Rom 11: 22-27)

In that day which God *"makes"*, the day of fulfilling the promises made. That day will include deciding between the *"righteous and the wicked"*. (Rev 20:11-15)

4:1-4   The Day of the Lord and the Second Coming of Christ is the *"great and terrible day"* mentioned in Joel 2:31. It is the *"day cometh"*, and may have a partial reference to the destruction of Jerusalem in 70 AD, but cannot only be that event, as it calls for a day of no escape and utter destruction.

"The sun of righteousness" has the idea of "righteousness as a sun", as being refined by fire. Most commentators believe it is better to understand it personally of Christ, and the consummation of salvation that He brings to those who are His.

"You shall tread down the wicked" is referenced by Fausset; "The righteous who shall be the army attending Christ in His final destruction of the ungodly (Micah 7:10; Zech 10:5; 1 Cor 6:2; Rev 2: 26, 27)."

The Jews are challenged to *"remember the Law"* as given by Moses, since Malachi was the last prophet for 400 years.

Malachi

4:5, 6   The final two verses of the Old Testament provide an intriguing promise that God will send Elijah to come before the Day of the Lord.

Christ said that John the Baptist fulfilled both of these prophecies in Malachi (3:1 and 4:5), and that he was the forerunner meant in each of them. (Matt 11:10-16; Luke 1:3; 11-17)

The Jews hold that a literal, personal Elijah was meant by Malachi in 4:5, and that it refers to Christ's first coming, and therefore they say Christ has not yet come because the literal, personal Elijah has not yet come.

Most modern commentators teach this prophecy has a double fulfillment; that John came *"in the spirit and power of Elijah"* before Christ's first coming, but the real, literal, personal Elijah will come before the Second Coming of Christ. Jesus said in Matthew 17:10, *"Truly Elijah shall first come and restore all things"*.

These words refer to a future and Second Advent of Christ. The natural inference is that he will be a real, personal Elijah, who effects reconciliation between the unbelieving children and their godly believing ancestors. The bond of union of the Jewish peoples, which had been broken, will be restored. (Mark 9:11-13)

Wycliffe closes the Old Testament commentary with this thought:

"Elijah did come and did make ready a people prepared for the Lord, and the Lord Jesus did come to His temple. So, although the Old Testament closes with a conditional curse, the New Testament ends with the unconditional promise of Christ coming for His own, *"Surely I come quickly"*, together with the answer to those who are His "peculiar treasure", the Jewish people.

"Even so, come, Lord Jesus."

The New Testament

Matthew   Written by Matthew (Levi), the publican. As early as 37 AD

The Gospel written as "Matthew" was primarily for the converts to Christianity from Judaism, who numbered in the thousands in the early Church. There is more frequent use of Old Testament Scripture quotations (93) than in any of the other Gospels. Much attention is given to Jesus fulfillment of Messianic prophecy, and thus Israel's Messiah, who would establish the promised kingdom. - Wycliffe

10:23   Jesus is giving instructions to His disciples as they are sent out *"to the lost sheep of Israel"*. In this discourse He is discussing that the *"kingdom of heaven is near"*, and this is the message the disciples are to deliver to those who will listen. He gives warnings about mistreatment they will receive on His account, as many reject Him. "This verse is the first reference that Christ ever made to His coming in any other sense than that of His presence with them in the world at that time." - Campbell Morgan

While there are various interpretations of this verse, it is mostly considered a reference to the Destruction of Jerusalem in 70 AD, which ended the old dispensation and is a type of the final coming of the Lord. Not even yet in the current time have the followers of Christ gone through all the cities and villages of Israel.

12:18-20   The end time judgment upon the Gentiles is meant here. Practically all scholars are agreed that by *"declaring judgment to the Gentiles"* the reference made here is to Christ as judge at the day of judgment. His judgment is to end in victory in the day of final decision, so that no further conflict will remain.
(Rev 20:11-15)

13:31, 32   The Kingdom of Heaven is like a mustard seed, small at the beginning, then becoming large. This portrays the growth of Christianity from small beginnings, then its increase and growth into a kingdom of great power that draws people and nations to it. This has certainly been seen over the centuries, and will be finally and fully concluded at the beginning of the *"new heavens and the new earth"*. (Rev 21:24)

13:37-43   The parable of the *"tares"*, or weeds, in verses 24-30 is explained here, as contrasted between the *"sons of the kingdom"* and the *"sons of the evil one...the enemy that sowed them is the devil."* *"The harvest is the end of the age and the harvesters are the angels."*

The reference is to the end of the period of time in which we are now living and to the Second Coming of the Messiah and His judgment. In verse 30; *"let both grow together"* tells us that there is to be a mixture of good and evil until the end of time. Then shall the evil ones be *"cast into the furnace of fire"*, and *"the righteous shall shine forth as the sun in the kingdom of their Father."* (Matt 24:31; 25:41; Rev 20:15; Dan 12:1-3)

13:44-46   These two parables portray the kingdom of heaven as a desirable treasure to possess. The *"treasure hidden in a field"* shows the condition of joyful and total surrender to obtain it. The *"pearl of great price"* is Christ Himself found by the one seeking truth.

13:47-50   The kingdom is like a dragnet, catching and separating the holy from the unholy. The parable teaches the development side by side of good and evil in the Church, and the world. *"So shall it be in the end of the world..."*. (13:37-43)

16:27, 28   The coming of the Lord foretold. These verses proclaim the glory of Christ at His Second Coming as judge, and His attendants shall be His angels. (Rev 19:14) There are some difficult things to understand in verse 28, and a variety of understandings by commentators. The statement that, *"There are some who stand here, who shall in no wise taste death, till they see the Son of Man coming in His kingdom"*, has been identified as Jesus *"transfiguration"*; His resurrection; the Holy Spirit at Pentecost; and His coming in the Parousia at the end of this age. All have flaws that seem to disqualify these interpretations.

Still other commentators refer the expression to the time of the Destruction of Jerusalem in 70 AD (10:23) as a type and an earnest of the final Second Coming of Christ.

19:27, 28   The disciples designated to judge Israel at the Lord's return is their *"reward"* in the *"regeneration"*. The whole world is to be restored to its original state of perfection (Isa 65:17) at the coming of Messiah, and the disciples are to judge the twelve tribes of Israel. This seems to best be considered, "A literal fulfillment in the future, and a full understanding lies beyond the veil", says Ellicott. (Luke 22:28-30)

21:43, 44   The rejection of the Jewish nation as *"the kingdom of God shall be taken away from you"*. Jesus plainly announces their rejection by God, and the kingdom *"shall be given to another nation"*. This other nation

Matthew

is not identified, and various ideas are expressed as to its meaning. Some think the Church is meant, while others believe that all future subjects of the kingdom, including Gentiles and the believing Jewish remnant, are being referred to here.

Could the nations founded on Biblical and Christian principles be meant? Could this *"nation bringing forth the fruits thereof (the kingdom fruits)"*, be in these last days assigned the task of worldwide evangelism? Most of the world evangelism done today comes out of the nations formed with a Biblical Christian world view, even as they decline into nations of apostasy and rebellion to the things of God. Such seems to be the times in which we now live...

Verse 44 is no doubt a reference to Daniel 2. The idea is, whoever falls on Christ, stumbles over Him as a "rock of offense" (1 Pet 2:8; Isa 8:14, 15), in the days of His humiliation and shall be broken. To fall over Him at His Second Coming is to incur His wrath and utter destruction. (Matt 25:31-33; Rev 20:15) Whatever the actual meaning, this much is clear; it is dangerous to encounter this stone and provoke it!

23:39   The glad welcome of the Lord at His Second Coming, when the repentant remnant of the Jewish nation shall recognize Jesus as their Messiah, and will turn with true and loyal Hosannahs and blessing to greet *"Him whom they have pierced"*.
(Deut 4:30, 31; Isa 66:20; Hos 3:4, 5; Zech 12:10; 14:8-11)

Chapter 24 - The Olivet Discourse - Signs of the end of the age.

These are the most important verses to study with all prophetic Scriptures, and apply to develop a proper understanding of His return. It must be remembered that we have here only a partial report of this discourse by Jesus, and even when taken with the accounts in Mark and Luke, it is quite probable that only a fraction of all that Jesus said has been preserved for us. (John 21:25) Even so, God has revealed that which we need to be prepared for the *"end of the age"*. (2 Tim 2:13; 3:16, 17; 2 Pet 1:16, 19-21)

These are difficult verses to exegete intelligently without knowing whether Jesus was speaking about the coming Destruction of Jerusalem in 70 AD, or about His Second Coming at the Parousia (meaning "presence"). Many expositors think the Lord is describing not one event, but two.

The challenge to understanding this discourse is to discern how these events have played out to date, and how they fit with much other prophetic Scripture.

24:1-3   The temple destruction foretold, and the two questions asked by some of the disciples. There are only two questions here: They wanted to know *"when"* the destruction foretold would take place; and then they wanted to know the *"sign"* of two things: His coming; and, the end of the world, which these two things, in their mind, were obviously to occur at the same time.

The first question relates to the destruction of the temple, as announced here by Jesus. The event occurred in 70 AD, by the Roman armies under the command of Titus. This war (66 AD - 70 AD) resulted in the slaughter of an estimated over one million Jews, and their subsequent dispersion. This effectively ended the nation of Israel at that time, until it was reestablished as a new Israel on May 14, 1948. Reference Isaiah 49:17-26 and Ezekiel 37:11-14.

In Luke 21 the only question asked was regarding the temple destruction, which occurred at the time of the Destruction of Jerusalem, and Jesus answer is practically the same as found here in Matthew, except in Luke 21:20-24 the Destruction of Jerusalem is referenced.

The second question: *"The sign of thy coming."* The word here is "parousia", meaning presence, and is the ordinary expression for the coming of the Lord. It never, in the New Testament, signifies anything else than the bodily presence, and the Destruction of Jerusalem is never implied by this term. "Parousia" is synonymous with *"appearing"* (1 Tim 4:14) and *"His revelation"*. (1 Cor 1:7)

24:4-14   The course of this present age (now some 2000 years) seems to be summarized in these verses. While some aspects could relate to the Destruction of Jerusalem, nowhere in this discourse, as recorded by Matthew, is there a word about Jerusalem, or the destruction of the temple. The account in Luke 21:20-24 gives the direct answer from Jesus to the question the disciples asked about *"when"* the temple (and Jerusalem) would be destroyed.

Verse 5   *"Many shall come in my name, saying, I am the Christ"*, claiming to be the Messiah. History records no such pretenders before the Destruction of Jerusalem, but there may have been. In more recent times there have been numerous pretenders making such claims.

Matthew

Verse 6   *"Wars and rumors of wars"* - Lange says, "All wars are meant down to the Parousia." History records no such wars prior to the Destruction of Jerusalem. *"But, the end is not yet."* No doubt here is meant *"the end of the age"*.

Verse 7   *"For nation shall rise against nation...there shall be famines and earthquakes in diverse places."* While these events and calamities have occurred throughout the centuries, the Twentieth Century produced two great world wars composed of many nations from throughout the globe, and there have been nations warring against each other continually, especially in the latter half of that century, and continuing to the present time. Tens of millions of people have been slaughtered. Famine continues in various places, and the incidence of major earthquakes has been increasing rapidly over the past 100 years. (See earthquake report below.)

Verse 8   *"The beginnings of travail."* There will be more severe events and pain to follow.

A Report About Worldwide Earthquake Activity
      - Data from U. S. Geological Survey

The following data is on the USGS website, and when I looked at it I was stunned to see the abrupt change in activity beginning in 2002. The data from about 1700 forward should be fairly inclusive, and of course the data from about 1900 forward should be very accurate.

Most records are for significant earthquakes above 5.0 scale, with most above the 6.0 level. The largest magnitude quakes ever known are as follows:

1952, Kamchatka, 9.0.   1960, Chile, 9.5;
1964 Alaska, 9.2;   2004, Sumatra, 9.1;
2010 Chile, 9.2

Note that they have occurred in the past 60 years. The 2010 disastrous earthquake in Haiti was in the 7.0 range, and over 230,000 people lost their lives. 2010 proved to be one of the most active earthquake years ever recorded.

Number of significant earthquakes as recorded by the USGS:

Totals: 1600's....... 9   1700's....... 14   1800's....... 60
        1900's....... 425

        2000 - 2009...... 421+   2010 183

Verse 9   *"Then"* - Here begins, in its most natural meaning, a chronological sequence of events given by Jesus, that leads to *"the end of the age"*. While there is some debate in this regard, the difficulties of understanding and relating these passages to other prophetic Scriptures can be resolved with less difficulty when taken in their most natural and literal sense.

"Then, shall they deliver you up unto tribulation...kill you...hated of all the nations for My names sake." Lange says, "Certainly this must refer to religious persecutions of modern times, as well as those of earlier times, the disciples being representatives of all Christians." The persecutions seem to be somewhat progressive, culminating in a worldwide environment of complete hatred and rejection of Christianity. (Mark 13:13) This, spoken by Jesus, indicates a time coming when Believers will be *"hated"* and *"killed"* as a result of their devotion to Jesus. Reference Revelation 17:1-6.
(1 Pet 4:12-19; Dan 7:21, 22; Luke 6:22; Rev 6:9-11; 7:13, 14)

Verses 10-12   *"Then"*, the chronology sequence continues as *"at that time many will turn away from the faith."* Many "Christians" will renounce Christ and become apostate because of persecution, false teachings, ridicule and the delayed coming of the Lord.

The apostates will *"deliver up one another"*; betray and hate those Believers who hold to the faith and Biblical revelation. Their actions will be spurred on by *"false prophets/teachers"* who *"lead many astray"* and cause *"wickedness to increase"*.

This turning from the faith, and deception by false teachings, is becoming more apparent as time goes on. There is much false teaching in the Church today, as a Scripture denying, liberal, social, okay to sin, "feel good" gospel, is replacing the Gospel of repentance from sin, salvation, and commitment to the leadership of Christ in the life of the Believer. (2 Peter 2)

Matthew

Doubtless the majority living at the time of the Second Coming will be numbered among these; *"the love of most will grow cold."* Jesus said to the last church (Laodicea) in Revelation 3:15-17, *"I am about to spit you out of my mouth. You say, 'I am rich'...but, you are wretched, pitiful, poor, blind, naked."* (Mark 13:13; 1 Tim 4:1-5; 2 Tim 3:1-5; 4:3, 4; 2 Pet 3:17; 2 Thess 2:3, 10, 11)

Verse 13   *"But, he who stands firm until the end will be saved."* The result of endurance by the faithful Believer *"until the end"* will provide deliverance. To the end of what? Most naturally this refers to the period of which the Lord was speaking, the end of the age. This then, would mean deliverance which comes to the faithful who go through all, or a portion, of the Great Tribulation. There is a discipline and rebuke by God on His children that comes when there is unfaithfulness and rebellion. (Heb 12:1-8) This is seen throughout Scripture. (2 Thess 2:3; Rev 6:9-11, 17; 11:13-19; 1 Thess 4:16; 5:9; Dan 12:1; Matt 24:30, 31)

Verse 14   *"The Gospel of the Kingdom"*, the Gospel of Christ, the Gospel of the Messianic universal kingdom, *"will be preached in the whole world as a testimony to the nations"*. This preaching is now going on throughout the world. In fact, it is not possible to know when this witness is complete. Even at Pentecost when the Gospel was preached there were present *"devout men out of every nation under heaven"*. The nations present, most likely represented those of the then civilized world, as known at that time. Also, the disciples *"went forth and preached everywhere"*.
(Acts 8:4; Mark 16:20)

Presently the whole world is covered by satellite TV, radio, films, videos and writings. Christian broadcasting and thousands of missionaries are constantly at work sharing the Gospel. Even in the closed Moslem countries tens of thousands are being converted to the saving Gospel of Christ. There is little of the whole world that does not have the opportunity to become acquainted with the facts about the Gospel, about Jesus and His resurrection, and His offer of grace for repentance, reconciliation to God and salvation. (Rev 14:6, 7)

"Then, (after the worldwide testimony) *shall the end come."* This is meant as the *"end of the age"*; the end of the troubles and tribulations that are to precede the Second Advent of Jesus Christ.

24:15-22   This section signifies a transition to the announcement of a greater calamity, perhaps with a two event meaning. Many expositors believe these verses refer to the Destruction of Jerusalem in 70 AD, while others refer them to the Great Tribulation.

Verse 15   This seems to connect what follows with that which went before as something following a natural sequence. *"When"*, is a designate of time, such as; at what time; at a time that; at which time; the time or occasion. *"Therefore"*, means "as a result of that".

The subject is *"the abomination of desolation"*. What is the "abomination of desolation", as meant here? There are several views:

1. At the Destruction of Jerusalem the Roman army caused this abomination by planting their standards on sacred soil. This is an extremely weak position since there is no religious character to it, as the term "abomination" is a reference to supplanting and ridiculing the Jewish worship of the Lord.
    (2 Thess 2:3, 4)

2. There are other expressions and views, but they also are difficult to defend.

3. Those who refer the passage to the time of the Parousia, which is connected to the Great Tribulation, refer the expression to the Antichrist of 2 Thessalonians 2:4. It is under his rule that the Great Tribulation is to take place. (Dan 9:26, 27; 11:31-37; 12:11)

Verse 16   Those in the city were to get out, and those out of the city in Judah round about were not to enter the city, but to flee also. The event to see and cause the fleeing is the abomination of desolation, *"spoken of through the prophet Daniel"*. In the Destruction of Jerusalem time these verses provided motivation for many Christians to leave and go to Pella. (Luke 21:20)

At the midpoint of the Great Tribulation the Antichrist will set himself up as the one to be worshipped in the temple in Jerusalem. (Dan 12:1-13; Rev 13:1-8) This also, is a warning and announcement to those living in Israel today. Soon there will be a rebuilding of the Third Temple in Jerusalem, and a renewal of the sacrifices for a short while, before Antichrist is revealed. Antichrist will desecrate this temple. (2 Thess 2:1 - 8)

Matthew

The Third Temple, also known by some as Ezekiel's Temple, is a religious notion and desire in Judaism rooted in the Bible. This desire is expressed in many of Judaism's prayers for the return and rebuilding of the Temple in Jerusalem that had once stood as the First (Solomon) and Second (Herod) Temples that were destroyed by the Babylonians, and later the Romans in 70 AD.

Since the destruction of the Second Temple in 70 AD, religious Jews have expressed their desire to see the building of a Third Temple on the Temple Mount. Prayer for this is a formal part of the Jewish tradition of thrice daily Jewish prayer services. Though it remains unbuilt, the notion of, and desire for a Third Temple is sacred in Judaism, particularly Orthodox, as an unrealized place of worship. The prophets in the Old Testament called for its construction, to be fulfilled in the Messianic era.

Unused ancient Jewish floor plans for a Temple exist in various sources, notably in Chapters 40–47 of Ezekiel (Ezekiel's vision predates the Second Temple) and in the Temple Scroll discovered in 1947 at Qumran among the Dead Sea Scrolls.

According to American fundamentalist Christian author Hal Lindsey, the Third Temple could be built right next to the Dome of the Rock. He believes, based on the theory of Dr. Asher Kaufman regarding the location of the Eastern Gate, that the Dome of the Rock was built on what the Bible refers to as the Court of the Gentiles. He states that according to Revelation 11:1, 2, the rebuilding of the Third Temple was not to include the part of the Temple Mount referred to as the Court of the Gentiles.

As part of its ongoing effort to prepare for a future rebuilt Temple, the Temple Institute in Jerusalem has been preparing ritual objects suitable for Temple use. Many of the over ninety ritual items to be used have already been made by the Temple Institute.

As of June 2008, a major project of the institute is the creation of the sacred uniform of the High Priest, and for the ordinary priests. This project, the culmination of years of study and research, has been underway for several years. The High Priest's Breastplate and Ephod have already been completed. The golden crown of the High Priest, was completed in 2007. The Temple Institute is also designing the garments for the lay priests.

- wikipedia.com

See "templeinstitute.org" for more information on their efforts.

Verses 17-20   The admonition to get out of the city is immediate. There is no time to spare, as events will transpire very quickly. It will be a calamitous and difficult time. On the Sabbath day travel restrictions may be in place.

In the war of the Destruction of Jerusalem it is a fact that over one million Jews were slaughtered. Over six million Jews were murdered in the Holocaust during World War II. There is today a threat against the Jewish people and nation of Israel to be "wiped from the face of the earth". This is the stated goal of the radical Islamist, lead by Iran.

Verse 21   Again, there is the *"then"*, that indicates a continuation of the sequence of events being foretold by Jesus. *"For then, there will be great tribulation, such as has not been from the beginning of the world until now, no, nor ever shall be."* There can be no doubt that here is stated a sequence of events that leads to the great end times tribulation period.

The Great Tribulation is a time of unprecedented calamity, a final one-time event that transpires over a several year period. The worldwide events of war, rumors of wars, famines, earthquakes, severe weather, etc., that precede the final seven year tribulation period will be but a prelude of the horrors to come.

Verse 22   If God did not intervene during *"those days"* of destruction, all of humanity would be destroyed. His grace and love for *"the elect"* causes Him to shorten the number of days of tribulation. This can only refer to *"the end of the age"*.

Verses 23-28   Jesus foretells of false Christ's and false prophets to come. The narrative, no doubt, begins to point now more to the future Second Coming than to the Destruction of Jerusalem, if to the Destruction of Jerusalem at all.

"Then", or *"at that time"* refers to what has just been prophesied, that is *"those days"* of the previous verse. The events will provide opportunity for false Christ and false prophets to demonstrate *"great signs and wonders"*. These are miracles performed by Satanic agencies as in 2 Thessalonians 2:9. Jesus advises to *"believe it not"*, for His Second Coming will be from the sky above, while these false ones are here on earth (verse 27).

Matthew

"If possible" even *"the elect"* would be deceived by these lying and false Satanic agents. This is strong evidence for the presence at this time of Believers, and their awareness and readiness of the soon Second Coming. (1 Thess 5:1-6; 2 Thess 2:3)

The openness of Jesus Second Coming is a universal observation as contrasted with the secrecy and deception of Satan and his false agents. Jesus presence (Parousia) is as *"lightening that comes from the East is visible in the West"*. The whole world will be illuminated and no one can mistake the actual event of His Second Coming in Glory.

Some commentators suggest the coming Son of Man will be suspended in the heavens while the earth makes one revolution! Every eye will behold Him (verse 30).

Verse 28   Has a variety of possible meanings. Christ is coming in judgment, and the spiritually dead are doomed to Messianic destruction, is perhaps as good an explanation as any.

Verses 29-31   The return of the King in Glory is further explained by Jesus. These are difficult verses to fully understand, as there are numerous scholarly interpretations.

Considering a more direct, simple and literal explanation, the following seems to best reveal what is referenced here about the Parousia of Christ in the end time.

The Wycliffe Bible Commentary summarizes it very well:

"(29): *"Immediately after the tribulation of those days"* - No reference is made here to the rapture of the Church.

(1 Thess 4:16, 17) Rather, the words describe the actual return of Christ at the end of the Tribulation and establish the Messianic reign. The accompanying astral phenomena are foretold also in Joel 3:15 and Isaiah 13:9, 10.

(30): *"The sign of the Son of Man"* is an identification whose appearance will cause the Jews (all tribes) to mourn as they recognize their Messiah (Zech 12:10-12). *"Clouds of heaven...power and great glory"* describe the same scene in Daniel 7:13, 14; 2 Thessalonians 1:7, 9.

(31): The angels who gather *"His elect"* are the same as described in Matthew 13:30, 41-43, as removing the tares from the wheat, that the wheat might then be gathered into the barn."

Gaebelein, Scofield, and others, find no reference at all in this entire chapter to the Destruction of Jerusalem, but refer it all to the final Parousia at the Second Coming. In Matthew the Lord says not a word about Jerusalem, or the destruction of the temple; while in Luke we hear that Jerusalem is to be besieged by armies, the inhabitants falling by the sword and *"led away captive into all the nations"*. Jerusalem is to be trodden down by the Gentiles. This is what occurred at the time of the Destruction of Jerusalem by Titus and the Roman army. (Luke 21:20-24)

Verse 31   Seems to provide a picture of either the "rapture" of His elect at this time, or another "collection", or gathering of His elect by angels. Some commentators refer this "gathering" to be the Jews in Palestine who are saved during the Great Tribulation. This is difficult because the passage clearly states the elect will be gathered *"from the four winds"* and *"from one end of heaven to the other"*. God's appointed time of fulfillment here is not perfectly known.

Referring to verse 30, Jesus said, *"at that time"*, which includes the activity described in verse 31. In the context He was referring to the events of the Great Tribulation, as in verse 29. It is not necessarily a 24 hour day, but a longer period of time of great distress and earthly upheaval that will cause *"men to faint from terror"*. (Luke 21:26)

At some point during the Great Tribulation Jesus will come *"with a great sound of a trumpet"*, and rescue His faithful Believers from the *"wrath of God"*. (1 Thess 5:9; 1 Cor 15:50 - 53; 2 Thess 1:6 - 10)

When is this trumpet sounded? Again, there are various ideas. Scofield and others argue that the trumpet is sounded at the close of the Great Tribulation, and at the beginning of the Millennium. Others argue for it being sounded at the time of the first resurrection of Believers (1 Thess 4:16; 1 Cor 15:52). Even others call for the trumpet at the general resurrection at the end of the Millennium.

Which is it? One, all, or none of the above? What does the Scripture tell? In the Revelation there is the vision of the Seven Trumpets. Seven is the

Matthew

number of completeness, of perfection, and of dispensational fullness, according to Wycliffe. The vision is found in Revelation 8:2-11:16.

The first four Trumpets introduce judgments that relate to the world of nature: earth's flora; sea; rivers and waters; celestial disturbances. The Fifth Trumpet, the First Woe, seems to be a great outburst of spiritual evil which shall aggravate the sorrows of the world. It is a picture of the bitter bondage of Satan upon humanity. The Sixth Trumpet, the Second Woe, relates to the River Euphrates, a literal geographic location. Four evil angels are unbound and released to kill a third of humanity. This fearful destruction seems to be brought about by huge armies of calvary. (Rev 9:16)

Wycliffe says, "Surely we here have come to the days of the beginning of Antichrist. This commences the last great struggle between the princes of the world and the people of God." There is no Scriptural evidence that these tumults cause a turning of mankind to God, or repentance, but a stubborn continuation of sin.
(Rev 9:20, 21)

The Seventh Trumpet announces the *"Kingdom of our Lord and His Christ"*. (Rev 11:15, 16) It is this last trumpet that introduces *"no more delay, but in the days when the seventh angel is <u>about to sound his trumpet</u> the mystery of God will be accomplished, just as He announced to His servants and prophets"*. (Rev 10:5-7)

Note that the mystery of God is to be accomplished *"in the days when the seventh angel is <u>about</u> to sound his trumpet"*. The trumpet sounds after, or during, the mystery accomplishment. Exactly how this works, and its timing, is not now fully understood.

The literalness of this, and the ancient prophecies actual fulfillments is to be finally and fully accomplished, and the whole world is to come under one powerful universal *"Kingdom of our Lord"*. (Eph 1:9, 10) God's wrath has come. The time has come for *"judging the dead...and for destroying those who destroy the earth"*, and for *"rewarding your servants and prophets and your saints and those who reverence your Name..."*. (Rev 11:18)

To the Apostle Paul was revealed much about *"the mystery of God"*, and about the last trumpet event. In 1 Corinthians 15:51-53 Paul says, *"We will be changed - in a flash, in the twinkling of an eye, at the last trumpet"*. In 1 Thessalonians 4:15-17 Paul provides another reference to the rapture being *"with the trumpet call of God"*. He gives further detail about the timing of the rapture event in 2 Thessalonians 1:6-10 and 2:1-8.

24:32-44   The Second Coming to be sudden, and the exact time known only to the Father. The parable of the fig tree and it's fruit is a symbol of the harvest, and also, many believe, the nation of Israel. (Joel 1:6, 7; Hos 9:10) Jesus associated a revitalized nation of Israel with the approach of these eschatological events. - Wycliffe.

The time of these events would occur *"before this generation* (or race, kind, family, stock, breed) *passes away"*. Never was a nation so completely distinct as a race in all accuracy of meaning as the Jewish people. No doubt this parable refers to the Parousia. If the rebirth of the new nation of Israel on May 14, 1948, is the fulfillment here, then right now, *"He, (Jesus) is near, right at the door"*.

Verses 37-39   Here makes a comparison between the *"days of Noah"* and the time at *"the coming of the Son of Man"*. (Gen 6:5-12) For the people of Noah's time were living in thoughtless security and gross sensuality. It was a day of great wickedness, violence and self indulgence. Noah and his family were rescued from the flood judgment. They had been advised and were aware of, and prepared, for the event. So shall it be with the righteous at the time of the Parousia.
(Matt 24:13; 1 Thess 5:1-10; 2 Thess 2:3; 2 Pet 3:14-18)

Verses 40-44   Here is the gathering of the elect at this time, *"at the coming of the Son of Man"*. The Believer is told by Jesus to *"keep watch, because you do not know on what day your Lord will come"*. So it is in all of life; a person knows not the day of death, so must be continually prepared to meet Jesus. (Matt 24:46; Psa 89:48; 116:15)

24:45-51   A comparison between the watchful and careless servants. It is the Believers duty not to be idly cruising through life, but to be a watchful student, prepared and working in the world on behalf of Jesus. (James 2:14) The *"wicked man"*, the unbeliever, is not interested or watchful, and as a result remains unrepentant, unsaved and condemned to the *"place with the hypocrites, where there will be weeping and gnashing of teeth"*.

Matthew

"Hypocrites" possibly refers to one who professes Christ, but the reality of lifestyle, belief and service is false. (Matt 25:12)

25:1-13   The five wise and the five foolish virgins is a parable from the Jewish custom that bridesmaids should wait at the bridegrooms house while he brought his bride from her father's house, usually after sunset. Another view is that the bridesmaids were with the bride at her father's house, then they would travel to the bridegroom's house for the marriage supper.

"Then" refers to the period spoken of at the end of chapter 24, the coming of the Lord. The *"virgins"* refer to a wide variety of interpretations, most likely they represent the Jewish remnant in the Tribulation. - Wycliffe. Some will be prepared and ready for the arrival of the Messiah, and some will be unprepared.

The lamp oil is considered by many to be symbolic of the presence of the Holy Spirit. True Believers are in-dwelt with the Holy Spirit. There is some debate about what exactly this means.
(Matt 3:11; Acts 1:5; 8:15-17; 9:17; 11:15; 19:1-7)

In Lockyer's book, "All About the Holy Spirit", he comments; "In regard to the Holy Spirit, we are not to be 'imitators" of Jesus, as that is an action of human effort. We are to be "transformed", renewed, born again, by the indwelling Holy Spirit. The Holy Spirit is God's change agent. We are to be "possessed" by the Spirit of Jesus, *"to be My witnesses...to the ends of the earth."*
(Acts 1:8; Matt 28:19)

25:14-30   The parable of the talents represents active watchfulness, and using that capability which the Lord provides to each individual in a responsible way. The first two servants were equally diligent and doubled their capital.

They received their masters commendation and reward; *"Well done, good and faithful servant."*

Faithfulness is the virtue being examined. Higher responsibilities and privileges are a part of the reward, and a sharing of the Lord's joy. The latter servant did not use his talent, instead buried it in the earth. What he was given to use was taken away and he was *"thrown outside, into the darkness, where there shall be weeping and gnashing of teeth"*.

According to Wycliffe, this parable is associated with the time of Tribulation saints, Jew or Gentile. The believing remnant will be gathered to enjoy the Millennial blessings, but those then living who have no real belief in the Messiah will be removed (Ezk 20:37-42).

25:31-46   The judgment based on works, the separation of the nations, as represented by the sheep and goats. The same scene here, as in 24:30, 31, marking the coming of the Son of Man to end the Great Tribulation and usher in the Millennium.

"The Son of Man" - The Lord here identifies Himself as *"the Son of Man"* described in the vision by Daniel (Dan 7:13, 14). This is a proof text of His Divinity as He has authority from the Father to sit in judgment.

When this judgment takes place is mostly considered to be at the end of the Millennium, and is on both Believers and unbelievers. The wicked are conceived under the figure of *"goats"*, an animal considered worthless and stubborn. The *"sheep"* being on His right is a place of honor and acceptance.

In verse 34, here for the first and only time, Jesus gives Himself the name, *"the King"*. As King He acknowledges those *"blessed of My Father"*, and invited to *"inherit the Kingdom"*. Follows is a proclamation regarding the proper behavior of the Believer leading the New Testament life.

In the following verses a comparison is made of those who have rejected the New Testament life, rejected the Messiah, and are condemned *"into the eternal fire prepared for the devil and his angels"*. (Rev 20:15)

26:64   Jesus answers the High Priest by referring to His presence with God, and His coming again *"on the clouds of heaven"*. It was a solemn confirmation of the truth involved in the High Priest's question; *"Tell us if you are the Christ, the son of God."* In other words, Jesus said, "I am!" For this affirmation of who He was (is), the High Priest charged Him with *"blasphemy"*.

When Jesus declared His Divinity, and His Second Coming *"on the clouds of heaven"*, He was claiming to be the Messiah who was seen by Daniel in his vision (Dan 7:13, 14). When He returns at the time of the end *"every*

Matthew

eye shall see Him", as His return is visible to all. His coming will not be a secret event.
(Mark 14:62; Luke 21:27; 22:67-70; Acts 1:11)

28:16 - 20   The writings of Matthew conclude with what is called "The Great Commission". It is the "work" of the Believer. This work includes a lifestyle that produces "good" for other people, and the development of a Christlike character as lived by Jesus Himself, and further defined in the writings of the Apostles Peter, Paul, John and others in the New Testament. It is these testimonies and eyewitness accounts that ensure the validity of who Jesus was, and is. (Rev 1:8; 22:13)

Then Jesus came to them and said, *"All authority in heaven and on earth has been given to Me. Therefore go and make disciples of all nations, baptizing them in the name of the Father and of the Son and of the Holy Spirit, and teaching them to obey everything I have commanded you. And surely I am with you always, to the very end of the age."*

As Believers assigned such "work", it is imperative that we understand our task, and the shortness of time. In Lockyer's wonderful book, "All About the Holy Spirit", is this comment:

"The Holy Spirit cannot fill the life of the Believer if it is full of something else. If full of pride, prejudice, preconceived ideas or of worldly pleasures, we cannot be full of the Spirit. We must be a willing vessel, available to be saturated and filled so as to allow the expelling of sin and sinful desire. Mere nominal Christians are of little account to the devil. He can afford to let them alone, seeing their unscriptural life is not disastrous to his cause."

True Believers come with an honorable pedigree. Such is beautifully and wonderfully described by George Matheson in his "Voices of the Spirit".

"We have an ancestry which goes back beyond nature, beyond maternity, beyond the flesh. We have a pedigree which is older than the mountains, older than the stars, older than the universe. We are come from good stock; we are branches of a high family tree; we are the scions of a nobel house, a house not made with hands, eternal in

the heavens. Nature is the parent of our flesh, but the divine is the Father of our spirits, the Spirit of God hath made us, and the breath of the Almighty has given us life."

- Quoted from "All About the Holy Spirit"

Mark   Written by John Mark, attendant of Peter.   57 AD - 63 AD

4:26-30   The parable of the growing seed is found only here in Mark. It shows that the growth of the seed depends upon a mysterious power implanted by God within it, the workings of which is hidden from the human eye. The earth by itself causes the seed to sprout, grow and mature for the harvest. All of this occurs without mans ability to change the stages of the seeds development through which it must pass.

There are several interpretations of this parables meaning. Verse 34 says, *"When* (Jesus) *was alone with His own disciples He explained everything to them".* We don't know His explanation. Perhaps one of the better ideas is that Messiah planted His seed of belief and ethical living so that the moral activity of His Believers will produce a fitting harvest at His return. (Matt 24:31; 13:37-39; Joel 3:13)

8:38   Those who disown Christ will be disowned by Christ at His coming. This, no doubt, refers to His Parousia.
(Luke 9:26; 2 Thess 1:7-10)

9:1   Refer to comments on Matthew 16:28 and Luke 9:27.

11:10   As Jesus rode into Jerusalem on a donkey the people expected an immediate Messianic kingdom with the restoration of the throne of David. Many Jews of that time recognized Jesus as the expected Messiah, but they misinterpreted His role as a King, rather than as a Savior. (Acts 1:6-8)

Chapter 13   Refer to comments on Matthew 24 and Luke 21.

14:25, 62   See comments on Luke 22:16-18; Matthew 26:64.

Luke   Written by Luke, a Gentile physician.   63 AD - 68 AD

1:32, 33   Christ is announced to be King forever on David's throne. This announcement made to Mary concerning Jesus has never yet been fulfilled, but will be at the appointed time for His Second Advent and personal reign on earth. (Isa 9:6, 7) The angel definitely designates Him as the One to whom the throne of David is to be given. This is a description of His recognition as the Messiah. As Messiah He is appointed King. (2 Sam 7:11-13; Psa 2:7-9; 89:26-29) The unbelief of Israel postponed the fulfillment of these promises to a time in the future.

4:16-20   Jesus public reading from the scroll of Isaiah was an implication about the Second Coming. In reading the passage from Isaiah 61:1, 2, He omitted the words, *"And the day of vengeance of our God"*, since the immediate and first aspect of His mission was to proclaim *"the acceptable year of the Lord"*, as then beginning with Himself. The fulfillment of the latter part of the passage would come at His Second Advent.

9:26   Jesus declares that, *"when He comes"*, a reference to His Second Coming, He will not claim those who have disowned Him. He is coming in threefold glory; *"in His own glory, the glory of His Father, and of the holy angels"*. (Mark 8:38)

9:27   Refer to comments on Matthew 16:27, 28.

12:35-40   Be in constant expectation of, watchfulness and preparation for the Lord's coming. The idea is to be free of anxiety, but to be good, educated and looking, to be blessed as one of His servants.

What *"marriage feast"* is meant? Is he just away at a friends feast and will soon return? Is this the heavenly *"marriage feast"*, from which He comes to with His saints in the air? Jesus was teaching the disciples that His return might be long delayed, which of course, has now been about 2000 years. He always implied that He would come suddenly, but not necessarily soon.

13:35   Believers will be glad and welcome the Lord at the Second Coming. The *"desolate house"* must refer to the time of great persecution when the world events will be so awful, especially for the Christian Believer, that they will be begging for Christ to return. (Luke 18:7; Rev 6:9; 1 Thess 5:1-5; Dan 7:21, 25)

17:20, 21   The kingdom is presented by Jesus to the Pharisees in the sense of a present reality. They wanted to discredit and entangle Him with the claims for an external Messianic Kingdom to come. Jesus challenged them to understand that the kingdom was first to be a spiritual work, done *"within you"*, in the depths of the heart. The external manifestation will reveal itself at the Parousia of Messiah.

17:22-37   Jesus now begins to speak to His disciples of His kingdom as a coming reality, but to not be deceived into following false reports about Him. His coming again will not be in secret, but visible and bright as lightening. (Matt 24:23-28) The Lord's coming will be universal and instantaneous, as He is manifested in His glory for all the world to see. For verses 26-30 refer to Matthew 24:37-39.

Verse 31   *"In that day"* is doubtless referencing the catastrophe which immediately precedes the Parousia, as described in Matthew 24:29-31.

Verses 32-36   Also refers to the day of calamity as covering activities in the night (sleeping) and the day (grinding). Some commentators believe the Parousia will occur at night in Israel, which of course, will be day in the other hemisphere. (Matt 24:40, 41)

In verse 37 the disciples ask, *"Where, Lord?"* They wanted to know the place where the persons removed would be taken. The Lord's answer begs the question; He simply states that where the corruption of death is, there will be vultures to clean up the decay. (Matt 24:28)

The universality of the judgment on Jew and Gentile alike was difficult for the disciples to grasp. The Jews believed that all descendants of Abraham would participate in the Kingdom of the Messiah.

18:1-8   This parable of the persistent widow is only found here in Luke, and is addressed to His disciples. It follows naturally after the thought of what precedes about the Parousia.

The widow represents the Church, contending with her adversary, the devil. She needs relief, as in the final days of sorrow before the Second Coming.

We are *"not to faint"* (1Thess 5:17), but continue in prayerful hope without ceasing, to stop the adversary and see justice rendered for the elect. (Rev 6:9 - 11) Vengeance and justice will come *"speedily"* in the end, as the Second Coming event will be *"as lightening"*. (2 Thess 1:6, 7)

Luke

"When the Son of Man comes will He find faith on the earth?" Literally it is *"the faith"*. It is such a persistent faith as the widow had, faith in God as a righteous judge, who will execute proper justice at His coming. It is a sobering fact that the doubt about this faith being evident at the Saviors coming, is revealing of the great apostasy foretold about the end times. (2 Thess 2:3; 2 Tim 4:3, 4; 1 Tim 4:1; 2 Pet 3:3, 17)

19:11-27   The parable about the nobleman and the postponed arrival of the kingdom. A similar, but different parable is recorded in Matthew Chapter 25.

There continued to be an expectation of the disciples that the present journey to Jerusalem was for the purpose of revealing and setting up the Messianic Kingdom. The nobleman represents the Lord Jesus, who was, of course, going on a journey to heaven. The nobleman provided the same amounts of money to ten servants, with an expectation of return to be gained while he was away. It was a relatively small amount, given as a test of fidelity and faithfulness.

Verse 14 describes the resistance of the Jews to Jesus as Messiah, which still continues to this very day. In verse 15 He was made their King anyway! The parable speaks strongly of reward for faithfulness and the severity of the judgment that will fall on the enemies of Christ when He comes again. (Verse 27)

This seems a strong, sure and final judgment on the Jewish people for their rejection of Him as their Messiah. (Zech 13:7-9; Rom 9:30-10:4)

21:5-36   See also exposition on Matthew Chapter 24. The destruction of Jerusalem and the temple foretold. Some commentators believe that in this discourse Luke seemingly contemplates exclusively the Destruction of Jerusalem. Luke is writing to the Gentiles, and therefore does not mention the prophecy of Daniel, as is found in Matthew and Mark, but speaks merely of its fulfillment. Many Gentile Believers fled Jerusalem before its destruction based on these warnings in Luke (verse 20).

21:24   The devastating results of the Destruction of Jerusalem was not only the slaughter of the Jews, but the scattering of the Jewish people, *"led captive into all the nations"*. The whole world was now open to them, while the Holy City was now closed. At least a million Jews perished during this time, while ninety-seven thousand were taken prisoner and dragged into Egypt and her provinces.

Furthermore, *"Jerusalem shall be trodden down of the Gentiles, until the times of the Gentiles be fulfilled."* Here we have a period of time of indefinite duration, to be completed at an appointed time by God. Jerusalem came back under mostly Jewish control in 1967. To this very day it is a controversy among the Gentile nations about who is to control the Holy City.

The Jerusalem Law

Passed in 1980, was widely believed to have reaffirmed Israel's annexation of Jerusalem and reignited international controversy over the status of the city. However, there has never been an official act that has declared expanded East Jerusalem as having been annexed by the State of Israel. The position of the majority of UN member states is reflected in numerous resolutions declaring that actions taken by Israel to impose its laws, jurisdiction and administration on the whole of Jerusalem are illegal and have no validity.

The Jerusalem Law states that "Jerusalem, complete and united, is the capital of Israel" and the city serves as the seat of the government, home to the President's residence, government offices, supreme court, and parliament. United Nations Security Council Resolution 478 (Aug. 20, 1980; 14–0, U.S. abstaining) declared the Jerusalem Law "null and void" and called on member states to withdraw their diplomatic missions from Jerusalem.

The United Nations and all member nations refuse to accept the Jerusalem Law and maintain their embassies in other cities such as Tel Aviv, Ramat Gan, and Herzliya. The U.S. Congress subsequently adopted the Jerusalem Embassy Act, which said that the U.S. embassy should be relocated to Jerusalem and that it should be recognized as the capital of Israel. The Palestinian Authority sees East Jerusalem as the capital of a future Palestinian state. The city's final status awaits future negotiations between Israel and the Palestinian Authority.   - wikipedia.org

---

Luke

As this is written, in summer, 2010, there are meetings going on in Washington, DC, between the USA, Palestinian and Jewish leaders, with other Middle Eastern Moslem nations in attendance, for the stated purpose of dividing up Israel and Jerusalem to provide a "home for the Palestinians". A primary purpose is to "establish peace and security for the region". Israel strongly desires to live in safety. (Ezk 38:8, 9)

21:25, 26   It is here that Jesus moves beyond the Destruction of Jerusalem to simply stating what shall take place after the *"times of the Gentiles"* are fulfilled; what will take place before His Parousia.

These signs are to be taken literally, as at the time of His coming there will be great turmoil on the earth and in the heavens.
(2 Pet 3:7-12)

21:27, 28   See also Matthew 24:29 - 31. Most early, but not all, premillennial expositors make no provision for any period of time between the Lord's coming for His saints and His coming with them, and consequently refers the redemption of verse 28 and the elect of Matthew 24:31 to the saints in general, and not to the elect of Israel. The redemption is brought to the saints by the appearing at the Second Coming of their Lord. If this be the case, the rapture occurs near the end of the Great Tribulation period.

21:29 - 31   See also Matthew 24:32 The reviving of the Jewish nation is to be taken as a sign of the near approach of the Parousia of Christ. On May 14, 1948, the nation of Israel was reborn. The world events of these past six plus decades testify to the nearness of the Second Coming of Jesus, and all that entails. The Messianic Kingdom is to be established at the time of Christ's Parousia; *"the Kingdom of God is nigh"*.

21:32, 33   Refer to comments on Matthew 24:34, 35.

21:34-36   Jesus warns, be careful how you live your life, for there is to be a universal judgment, a universal surprise; *"that day will close on you unexpectedly like a trap"*. The admonition to *"always be on the watch"* is a serious challenge to the Believer to be so grounded as to be able *"to stand before the Son of Man"*. (Dan 7:1-28) The days of the Antichrist rule will test the True Believer. (Dan 7:25; Matt 24:9-13; Luke 18:1-8)

22:16-18   The Passover Feast is an image of the great Marriage Supper to come. Alford says the words of these verses carry on the meaning and continuance of its Eucharistic ordinance even into the new heavens and the new earth. It has not only a commemorative, but a prophetic meaning. Think of the time when He comes again to celebrate His Holy Supper with His own, new, in His Kingdom of Glory. (Matt 26:29; Mark 14:25; Rev 19:6-9; Luke 22:30)

22:28-30   The Lord acknowledges the disciples steadfastness with Him *"in my temptations"*. He speaks of His whole life as one of trial and temptation, and His Victory over sin and death results in the Kingdom from the Father being appointed unto Him. Likewise His disciples steadfastness earns for them a place in the Kingdom as *"judges of the twelve tribes of Israel"*.

22:67-70   Refer to comments on Matthew 26:64.

24:21   The resurrected Jesus joins two other men on the road to Emmaus (verse 13). They expressed disappointment regarding recent events in Jerusalem. They referred to the crucifixion of Jesus, and *"hoped that it was he who would redeem Israel"*. Redemption, in their minds, was for a political and religious deliverance.

Jesus opened the Scriptures and explained who He was in verses 25-27. See also verses 44-49. Jesus related the Old Testament Scriptures as being literally fulfilled, as He said, ***"How foolish you are, and how slow of heart to believe all that the prophets have spoken!"*** So it should be the same for us today, to *"believe all that the prophets have spoken!"*

John   Written by the Apostle John.   85 AD - 90 AD
             After the Destruction of Jerusalem.

5:21-29   The future resurrection that Christ is to accomplish is for both the righteous and the wicked. God, the Father, has appointed His Son, Jesus, to be the life giver, and the judge in the final days. It is plainly stated in verse 24 that Believers in God's Word about Jesus Christ, the prophesied Messiah of the Jews, *"cometh not into judgment"*. The question of the Believers title to heaven has been settled on the Cross, not at the bar of judgment. (Matt 25:31-46)

John

These passages argue for the case of one resurrection, or two. There are various ideas, primarily related to the timing of the resurrection(s). Are the righteous and wicked resurrected together, or at separate times during the final days?
(Psalm 1:5; Rev 20:5, 11-15; Dan 7:9, 10)

6:39, 40, 44, 54 The Believers bodily resurrection is set forth at the last day. These passages are beyond dispute. It is presented here as the necessary crowning of the spiritual work accomplished by Christ in the Believer. Meyer says, "It is the first resurrection that is meant, that to everlasting life of the Messianic Kingdom, and as a matter of course, it includes the transformation of those still living." (John 5:29; 1 Thess 4:13-17; 2 Thess 1:6-10; Rev 20)

The meaning of *"the last day"*. As is here stated must mean the time period of the rapture of the Church, as Meyer seems to indicate. The resurrection of the dead in Christ comes first, then the transformation of the living Believers follows immediately. (1 Cor 15:35-53; 1 Thess 4:13-17) This will occur *"in the twinkling of an eye, at the last trump"*. (Matt 24:31; Rev 11:15, 18)

If there is only one final resurrection, as some teach, then this must take place at the end of the Millennium. (Rev 20:11-15) If there are two resurrections, one for the Believers, and then one later for judgment (John 5:24-29), then this first resurrection must take place at, or near, the end of, on the *"last day"*, of the Great Tribulation. (Rev 20:4, 5) The latter seems the most plausible and confirmed by the most Scripture. The *"last day"* may, or may not, be a twenty-four hour period of time, and may occur over many *"days"*.
(2 Pet 3:8) Refer to commentary on Daniel 12.

11:23-26 Jesus promise to Martha about her brother Lazarus; *"Your brother shall rise again"*. She replied with the prevailing belief of the Jews of that day, *"I know that he will rise again in the resurrection at the last day"*. (Dan 12:1, 2) Jesus declared His personal power of both life and resurrection; the One who raises and who makes alive when He said, *"I am the resurrection and the life..."*. He goes on to say the Believer may physically die, yet live, and never die (in the resurrection).

14:1-6   Jesus declares He will come again, from the place He is going, His Father's house. While there He will prepare a place for the disciples, so they may be where He is also. Christ is speaking of coming to fetch them to a prepared place whose locality is determined. The reunion mentioned here is to be in heaven, rather than on earth. Jesus further declares himself to be *"the Way...that no one comes to the Father except through Me"*.

This claim is a great stumbling block for many, who believe and teach there are many paths to God. In verse 10 is the question all persons must face.

Verses 1-3 are used by some as proof of the pre-tribulation rapture. It is a view that is not easily proved by other Scripture. Yes, Jesus is coming to fetch the True Believer (rapture), but the uncertain answer is "when". Alford says, "The coming is begun in His resurrection (verse 18), carried on in the spiritual life (verse 23), further advanced when each in death is fetched away to be with Him, and fully completed at His coming in glory when they shall be with Him forever."

In context Jesus is comforting the disciples, as they are "troubled", especially Peter, whom Jesus has just said would deny him three times (verse 13:38). He is assuring them of a future with Him when they die, after He has departed to the *"place"* where He is soon going (verse 13:33).

There are those who see in these words a reference to the return of Jesus through the Holy Spirit at Pentecost, and thereafter abiding with them. This view is favored by the fact that the whole chapter deals with the coming of the *"Comforter"*.

Others reject this view, but it could be that two promises are contained in the words, and may not necessarily refer to the same time period. One time is at the death of the Believer, and the other at the Parousia if he is then still living.

14:15-18   Jesus promises *"another Counselor"* to come, the Holy Spirit, who is one with Christ, and will testify of Him. See also verses 23-29.

16:13   The Holy Spirit to be the revealer of things to come. Jesus calls the Holy Spirit *"the Spirit of Truth"* who will *"not speak of himself...and he will declare unto you the things that are to come"*. This was undoubtedly done through the Apostles writings, which have been preserved for us over

John

the centuries. (Acts 1:7, 8) Note that Jesus did not say the role of the Holy Spirit was to be a "restrainer" of evil, or of the Antichrist. (See comments on 2 Thess 2:7)

16:19-22   The coming of Christ through the Holy Spirit at Pentecost, is here predicted by Jesus. The grief of His departing in the Ascension would be replaced with the joy of the filling by the Holy Spirit at this event. The perfect consummation of this joy will occur at the Second Coming of Jesus in glory.

18:36   *"My Kingdom is not of this world."* His Kingdom does not emanate from this world, but from above.

21:21-23   The Second Coming and the death of John are in question here. What did Peter mean with his question, *"What shall this man do?"* He was referring to John, and was curious if the martyrdom he, Peter, was to experience applied to John also. (21:18-20) Jesus gently rebuked Peter by responding, *"What is that to thee?"* In other words, Peter, mind your own business! Devote yourself to following Me.

The idea, *"Tarry 'til I come"*, is a direct reference to the Second Coming, and at that time His Parousia was expected to be near. (Acts 1:6) Alford says, "At the Destruction of Jerusalem began the mighty series of events of which the Apocalypse is the prophetic record, and which is in the complex known as the 'coming of the Lord', ending, as it shall, with His glorious and personal advent."

The establishment, in full, of the present dispensation of the kingdom was initiated by the destruction of the nation, the temple, and the city of the Jews at Jerusalem, and the scattering of the Jewish people, as the beginning of the Parousia of Christ. His presence within the Believer will be consummated at His personal Second Coming.

The writings of John, as he recorded his personal experiences with Jesus in the flesh, and his recollections and revealings by the Holy Spirit, give us in this present time a small "peek" into the reality of what it means to "know Jesus". In John, Chapter 20, verses 29-31 is John's purpose in his writings:

"Then Jesus told him (Thomas), *'Because you have seen me, you have Believed; blessed are those who have not seen, and yet have Believed.'* Jesus did many other miraculous signs in the presence of His disciples, which are not recorded in this book.

"But, these are written that you may believe that Jesus is the Christ, the Son of God, and that by Believing you may have life in His Name." **John 20:31**

"For God so loved the world, that he gave His One and Only Begotten Son, that whoever Believes in Him shall not perish but have eternal life.

For God did not send His Son into the world to condemn the world, but to save the world through Him. Whoever Believes in Him is not condemned, but whoever does not believe stands condemned already because he has not believed in the Name of God's One and Only Son." **John 3:16 - 18**

Acts   Most likely written by Dr. Luke, shortly before the Destruction of Jerusalem.   65 AD

1:6-8   The followers of Jesus, after His resurrection, were looking for an immediate establishment of the Messianic Kingdom in Israel, *"at that time"*. Jesus had previously promised the Baptism of the Spirit would take place, and this was always connected with the coming of the kingdom. They were still confused about His purpose, and their destiny as His servants. In verse 7, Jesus answers them only as to time, *"It is not for you to know times, or seasons..."*.

The Apostles, most were to be less prophets of the future, and more witnesses of the past and recorders of their efforts as they were to establish the Church everlasting. As "witnesses" they were to proclaim His teachings, life, death, resurrection and ascension, to convince people of His purpose: salvation and life eternal, the forgiveness of sin and righteous living until He comes again. (1 John 2:15-17)

1:9-11   Jesus ascension and the promised return are vividly portrayed in these verses. Baumgarten beautifully says, "While the ascension of Elijah may be compared to the flight of a bird which none can follow, the ascension of Christ is, as it were, a bridge between heaven and earth laid down for all who are drawn to Him by His earthly existence."

Acts

He did not disappear, as He previously had on occasion, but He went visibly up to the Father in human form, and it is in this image that we make our prayers and petitions to Him.

He will return *"in like manner"*. He is coming again visibly and bodily, fast as lightening, so that people will see Him as He comes. (Matt 24:27; 2 Tim 4:8)

2:17-21   The beginning of the "last days" as the Holy Spirit is poured out at Pentecost (2:1-4). These verses are almost verbatim of Joel 2:28-32, and signify the age of Messiah, the period in which we now live. The *"age of the Messiah"* was called the "last days" because it was to be the last dispensation of religion.
(Isa 2:2; Micah 4:1; Heb 1:1-4; 2 Tim 3:1-5; 1 John: 2:18)

Verses 17, 18   Offer of the Spirit to *"all flesh"*. All Believers, without any distinction as to race, gender, or position, were to receive this special outpouring of the Spirit.

The Spirits presence provides ability to communicate religious truth in general, under divine inspiration, and the proclamation of the Word. (John 16:7-14)

Verses 19-21   "When great events are about to occur wonderful phenomena foretoken their appearance", says Hackett. The pronouncement of *"wonders and signs"* signify the very "end of days" that are coming on the earth. A day is at hand which will be one of thick gloom and sadness and woe.

This great prophecy in Joel will assuredly precede that awful day of the Lord's wrath. The promise of salvation still being available in these dark days is made, *"Everyone who calls on the name of the Lord will be saved."* See commentary on Joel 2:28-3:2.

2:29-36   Jesus is proclaimed by Peter as the heir to David's throne. This great proclamation shows the application of prophecy about David could only be to Christ. The Messiah of whom David was speaking and who was to sit *"upon his throne"*. The Messiah is *"by the right hand of God exalted"*. (Rev Chapter 5) God's mighty power is seen in the exaltation of Christ as well as in His resurrection, and *"the promise of the Holy Spirit"*.

In verse 36 Peter draws the conclusion from all that has been said; *"Let all Israel be assured of this: God has made this Jesus, whom you crucified, both Lord and Christ."* Such a definitive statement caused a great number of Jews to repent and become Believers (2:37-41).

Peter said, *"this Jesus"*. The heart of the Gospel is; *"this Jesus"*, raised from the dead and exalted at the right hand of God, has been made both Lord and Messiah. His Messiahship means Lordship; He reigns at the right hand of God as Lord and King.

The Lordship of Christ was the cardinal doctrine of primitive Christianity. Jesus entered into the exercise of His Lordship by virtue of His exaltation (Phil 2:9-11), and salvation is to be found in confessing Jesus as Lord. (Rom 10:9; Heb 1:1-4) - Wycliffe

Unfortunately today, many churches do not preach the Lordship of Christ in the Believer. They do not teach the validity of all Scripture and its full application in the life of the church and its members. (Heb 4:12) This watering down of Scripture truth and social commentary in many churches today is strong evidence of the "apostasy and falling away" predicted for the "end time".
(Luke 18:1-8; 2 Thess 2:3; 1 Tim 4:1; 2 Tim 4:3, 4; 2 Pet 2:1-3; 20, 21; 3:17, 18)

As you are reading this now, and if you have never accepted Jesus as your very own personal Savior, and made Him Lord of your life, why not now? The Scriptures make it plain:

Romans 3:10 - None are righteous;

Romans 3:23 - All have sinned;

Romans 5:8 - God loves us, while we were still sinners, Christ died for us (John 3:16);

Romans 6:23 - The wages of sin is death...the gift of God is eternal life in Christ Jesus, our Lord (John 8:24; 11:25);

Romans 10:9, 10 - If you confess with your mouth, "Jesus is Lord", and believe in your heart that God raised Him from the dead, you will be saved.

Acts

For it is with your mouth that you confess and are saved (John 3:35). By repentance of sin and belief in your heart, you become born again "in the Kingdom of God, through His Son, Jesus." (John 14:6) Be baptized in His Name. (Acts 2:38)

Find, and immediately become involved in a church that preaches and teaches the full truth of the Scriptures in the Holy Bible.

3:19-21   The Apostle Peter proclaims the seasons of refreshing and the restoration of all things as has been prophesied by God's holy prophets. The call to repent is to the Jews for their ignorance (3:17) so that their sin may be *"blotted out"* (erased). Repentance brings *"seasons of refreshing from the presence of the Lord"*.

At the point of repentance and belief a spiritual refreshing comes from believing in Christ, as one is "born again" into the everlasting Kingdom of God. (John 3:3)

See also comments below, as this refreshing may be related to the conversion of the Jewish nation during the Great Tribulation and consummated at Jesus Second Coming, when the Jewish people are anguished and repentant over seeing *"the one they pierced"*.
(Zech 12:10-13)

The *"seasons of refreshing"* strongly relates to the Second Coming as well. Alford says, "In this expression is clearly meant some future refreshment which the conversion of the Jews was to bring about." This passage may represent that the Second Coming is conditioned in the divine plan by the repentance of the Jewish nation, which includes the coming of Elijah, (Matt 17:11; Mal 4:5, 6) and the testimony of the 144,000 sealed Jewish witnesses of Revelation Chapters 7 and 14. Refer to commentary on Revelation 14:1-5.

There is some debate about the exact meaning of verses 20 and 21. Verse 20 plainly refers to the Second Coming of Jesus, and that in verse 21, *"He remains in heaven until the time comes for God to restore everything..."*. What then is to be restored? And when?

Several scholars offer the following idea: All that God has spoken through His holy prophets shall be restored and placed in its original order. It is a restoration to a state of primeval order at the Second Coming. It will be a moral restoration, good will overcome evil, etc. This restoration must be for the Millennium period (Rev 20:1-3). The Millennial restoration includes the nation of Israel to a place of authority and honor among the nations. (Jer 31; 33:6-9; Acts 15:14-18)

10:42　　　　Peter challenges the Jewish people to acknowledge the risen Jesus Christ as the One ordained by God as *"the judge of the living and the dead"*. (2 Tim 4:1; 1 Pet 4:5) This judgment comes at His Second Coming, and refers to the physically alive and physically dead, not the righteous and the wicked. (1 Thess 4:16, 17)

14:22　　　　The Apostle Paul advised that the Kingdom of God is entered through *"many tribulations"*. This was after he was stoned and left for dead. (14:19, 20) Wycliffe says, "The Kingdom of God is here the future eschatological realm established by the return of Christ in glory. In this age the Church must expect tribulation as it looks forward to the glory of the future Kingdom." Paul's exhortation to *"continue in the faith"* was, and is, a challenge to maintain the truth of the Gospel, and to not fall away due to *"many tribulations"*. (2 Tim 3:12; 1 Pet 4:13-19)

15:14-18　　　　Refer to Amos 9:11-15. The restoration of the Kingdom of David, and the calling of the Gentiles. God promised to restore *"the tabernacle of David, which is fallen"*, and make it flourish as in olden times, and to make the Gentiles a part of the theocracy. Scofield says, "This great passage has been aptly called 'the divine program of this age and the next'."

Attention must be called to the words 'take out' in verse 14. It is exactly what is to be seen; not the conversion of all, but the taking out, or from, the Gentiles, of some, *"a people for Himself"*.

After this taking out, Christ will return and then follows the conversion of the world. This ultimate conversion must occur at the end of the Millennium (Rev 21:24-27).

Romans   Written by the Apostle Paul.   60 AD

1:18, 19   In this most important letter Paul gives the reasons for the *"wrath of God"* against the *"godlessness and wickedness of men who suppress the truth by their wickedness, since what may be known about God is plain to them, because God has made it plain to them"*. In all of creation God's existence has been exhibited and *"clearly seen...so that men are without excuse."*

Paul continues this indictment for the next several chapters in Romans, and provides examples, illustrations and the plan for salvation through belief in Christ Jesus.

Lockyer, in his excellent writing, "All About the Holy Spirit", had this to say, "Ignorance is the sin of the saved. It effects the progress of Spiritual experience and proves a lack of knowledge."

Mankind learned from the *"Tree of Knowledge"* in Genesis 2 the difference between *"good and evil"*. In Psalm 119:66 a plea is made; *"Teach me knowledge and good judgment."* Proverbs 1:7 advises that, *"Fear of the Lord is the beginning of knowledge"*.

Proverbs contains much wisdom and "knowledge" advice. Proverbs, Psalms and other Scripture, were regularly read at the beginning of classes in schools across America until the readings were stopped in 1960's. This suppression of Biblical influence and wisdom resulted in the swift advancement of wickedness in future generations.

Hosea 4:1-6 declares a charge the Lord has against His people, the Israelites. It could be made against the world today, as well. Verse 6 sums it up very well, *"My people are destroyed from a lack of knowledge, because you have ignored the law of your God"*.

Jesus said to the men on the road to Emmaus, in Luke 24:25, **"How foolish you are, and how slow of heart to believe all that the prophets have spoken...".**

Jesus did not say, "some" of what the prophets have spoken, but *"all"*. Today it seems to be mostly not "all", but the "some", according to what people desire to hear (2 Tim 4:3). There is an ignorance that is the result of the unavailability of information. Then there is "willful ignorance". The choice is made to ignore the information, to not study and seek knowledge and understanding. Information about God and His Son are abundant in the world at this time. But, the rejection and false teaching about the Scriptures is also abundant.

The rejection of God's Word and ways is becoming more public and the rise of ridicule and persecution continues to swell and may soon overwhelm the True Believer, as prophesied. (Rev 7:9, 13, 14; and others)

8:16-25   The whole creation awaits the Second Coming of Christ. The children of God are *"heirs of God"* and *"joint heirs with Christ"*, and are to inherit the glorification promised by God at the Second Coming of Christ.

Not only are the sufferings and groaning's of humanity discussed here, but the *"creation itself also shall be delivered from the bondage of corruption"*. This occurs at the Apocalypse of Christ at the end of the present time, when the full redemption comes with the coming of the Lord Jesus at His Parousia, when the glory which is now hidden in heaven shall be revealed.

"The glory will not consist only in our own transformation, but also in the coming of the Lord Himself, and the transformation of the universe", - Godet. (1 John 3:2; Col 3:4; Rev 21:1)

Campbell Morgan says, "Creation is to be freed from its groaning and travailing in pain: the blight upon nature will be removed, and a perfect manifestation of its beauty will replace all it now suffers in company with fallen humanity."

Verse 23   *"First fruits of the Spirit"*, - Alford says, "The reference here is to the indwelling and influences of the Holy Spirit, as an earnest of the full harvest of His complete possession of us, body, soul and spirit, hereafter. Paul treats Him as an earnest and pledge given to us, and of His full work in us as the efficient means of our full glorification hereafter."

"The redemption of our body" means to be freed from all defects of its earthly condition. The Believer will be glorified into the incorruptible body similar to the glorified body of Christ. This occurs at the time of the Second Advent of Jesus Christ. (1 Cor 15:35-44; 51-53)

Verses 24, 25   *"For in this hope we are saved."* Paul always distinguishes faith and hope (1 Cor 13:13), and he always bases salvation on faith, from which hope precedes. The fact of salvation places the Believer in a condition of which hope is a characteristic. (Heb 6:17-20)

Romans

As a result of our faith *"we wait patiently for it"*. With steadfastness and patient endurance of the sufferings and tribulations (verse 18) of this present time, we hope for a glory yet to be revealed at the coming of the Lord. (John 16:33)

9:27-29   The words spoken from Isaiah 10:22, 23 about the return from captivity of a remnant of Israel. No matter how numerous the people of Israel might be, only a remnant of them are to be saved. Paul is here emphasizing the fact that only a remnant will be saved. The rescued Israelites are in Isaiah *"a holy seed"* (Isa 6:13), because out of them, as a small beginning, the nation shall rejuvenate itself.

Today, in the whole world there are only about fourteen million Jews, as compared to a world population of almost seven billion people. The number of Jews in Israel is about five and one half million. This tiny group of people command the attention of the whole world. Scripture says only one-third of them shall survive *"the end times"*. (Zech 13:7-9; Ezk 20:34-38)

11:5   Paul acknowledges that in his present time there is a remnant of the believing Jew according to the election of grace. There were many thousands of Jews who became Believers in the early church. (Acts 2:41; 21:20)

11:11-15   In these verses Paul shows God had a double purpose to open the gateway of salvation to the Gentiles, and to provoke the Jewish nation to jealousy and thus finally save them by His grace. Paul is speaking primarily to the Gentiles, as, *"I am an Apostle to the Gentiles"*. Even so, he strongly desired salvation for his own people. He apparently expected the conversion of *"all Israel"* at the Second Advent. This could mean the remaining Jews still alive at that time who witnessed Jesus return, and mourned *"the one whom they had pierced"*.

11:25-27   Paul here reveals *"this mystery"*. It was made known to Paul by revelation by God. This "mystery" reveals that Israel has fallen for an unknown period of time, *"until the fullness of the Gentiles"* be completed. The *"hardening in part"* has been a process whereby the whole nation became unbelieving, not just a part of it.

The Jewish people of today, whether in Israel or other locations, for the most part, are not "religious". They remain separate as a people, but unbelieving in practice.

How and when *"all Israel be saved"* is a debated question. Most likely the expression is to be taken numerically, not that every individual will be saved, but that the nation as a whole shall be.
(Isa 59:20, 21; 27:9; Jer 31:33, 34; Mal 4:5, 6)

13:11, 12   *"Knowing the season"*, is an expression of the general character of the time, as being awake or asleep. Some think Paul's expectation was for an immediate return of Jesus at His Second Advent. "But", says Alford, "because Paul in 2 Thessalonians 2 corrects the mistake of imagining it to be at hand or even already actually come, is no sign that he did not expect it soon."

Alford further says, "On the certainty of the event our faith is grounded; by the uncertainty of the time our hope is stimulated and our watchfulness is aroused." Paul, in 2 Thessalonians 2 also gives some specific events to precede the Second Coming so as to prepare the Believer to be watchful, understanding the times, and ready. (Matt 24:45-51; 25:12)

16:20   Here is revealed the swiftness with which this event, the final deliverance of the adversary, will be accomplished. The Greek word used here for *"shortly"* is "tachus", and denotes rapidness, not nearness, of the event. The victory will be speedily gained when once the conflict is begun.
(Matt 24:36-42; Mark 13:32-36; Luke 21:34-36)

This also applies to Revelation 22:20, *"I come soon"*. A better meaning is to say, "I move rapidly even though my arrival may be a great way off".

Genesis 3:15 is a prophetic assurance that the great adversary himself would be *"crushed"* at the Second Coming of Jesus, and all enemies shall be made the footstool of the Messiah and of His saints, through Him. (Heb 10:11-14)

16:25-27   Paul's doxology centers in God's ability and power to strengthen the readers. It is a *"proclamation of Jesus Christ"*, the Gospel preached by Paul and the revealing of the mystery that had been concealed, but now being revealed through the prophetic Scriptures (then the Old

Romans

Testament). The eternal purpose is *"so that all nations might believe and obey Him..."*. The eternal glory *"forever"*, of Christ Jesus will be accomplished at His Second Advent.

1 Corinthians Written by the Apostle Paul after he wrote the Thessalonian letters. About 55 AD

1:7, 8   Paul encourages the Believer to be confident while *"waiting for the revelation of our Lord Jesus Christ"*. There is here a recognition of Spiritual maturity in the Corinthian Christians. This maturity ensures strength that keeps the Believer patiently waiting for *"the day of our Lord Jesus Christ"*.

This is the decisive day of His Second Coming. This day as related to His Parousia is not quite the same as *"the day of the Lord"*. The former always relates to saints and their reward, while the latter relates to sinners and their punishment.

Erdman says, "The transactions associated with "the day of Christ" or "the day of our Lord Jesus Christ", in every Scripture where it is found, pertain exclusively to the risen and transfigured Church...but the events associated with "the day of the Lord", both in the Old Testament and the New Testament, concern especially the Jews and the nations of apostate Christendom, and are dark with the wrath of God upon the wicked."

3:13   The Believers Spiritual maturity and "works" are in discussion here. In 3:1-4, Paul admonishes those who professed Christ, but are still *"worldly"*, and causing difficulties in the Church by following a *"man"*, rather than being *"God's fellow workers"* (verse 9).

Here in verse 13 comes the warning that each persons "work" will not remain hidden, but be revealed *"for the day shall declare it...in fire"*. Most all commentators maintain *"the day"* being the Parousia of the Lord, the Second Advent. *"Fire"* may be a figurative term that denotes the judgments of the fruit of every man's ministry (2 Thess 1:8; 2 Pet 3:10-18), or the fire of judgment in which Christ will appear at His Second Advent (Rev 19:11-16).

4:5   Paul declares it is the Lord who judges him, and admonishes all Believers to refrain from judging him, as when the Lord comes all hidden things of darkness and the motives of a persons heart will be revealed. Whatever praise is earned is to be given by the Lord, not by man.

(In my personal experience the severe divisions in church have always been caused by a group of people giving exaggerated praise and allegiance to a pastor who encouraged such devotion to himself. These people follow a personality, rather than the Word.)

5:5   The Apostle Paul gives strong direction about what to do with an immoral person in the church. Excommunication, pure and simple. It is necessary that such a person be handed over to Satan to complete the *"destruction of the flesh"*, so that the person might repent and thus *"his Spirit may be saved in the day of the Lord Jesus"*.

Wycliffe says, "Inflated by false liberty, the church was puffed up. A church can never prevent evil absolutely, but it should always practice discipline. This severe action directed by Paul is to be remedial, as a bodily chastisement to restore the person (1 Cor 11:30; 1 John 5:16, 17)."

This discipline is sorely lacking in the Church at this present time. Gross sins, such as practicing homosexuality, unmarried persons living together, etc., are in some places of worship given hearty approval, as "false liberty" is openly proclaimed. (Rom 1:21-27)

It is clearly revealed in Scripture that bodily afflictions are often, but not always, caused by the agency of Satan, and it is also clear that the Apostles were invested with the power of miraculously inflicting such evil afflictions (5:3).
(Acts 5:1-11; 13:9-11; 1 Cor 10:8; 12:10)

6:2, 3   Saints are declared to sit in judgment on the world, and angels as well. Paul taught the early church doctrines, and here seems a reminder of things previously taught. What was said in Matthew 19:28 of the Apostles is here extended to the saints in general, and Paul is speaking of such judicial work of the saints as is ascribed to them in Daniel 7:22.

There is some dispute among scholars as to the time when the saints sit in judgment; is it at the last judgment, a judging with Christ during His

1 Corinthians

Kingdom of Millennial reign? As far as *"judging angels"*, the majority say this refers to "bad angels".

7:29-31   *"The time is shortened"* - means "time" compressed, contracted, brought within narrow limits. The idea here is related to the great prophecy of the Lord, which is key to this chapter (Luke 21:8, 9; Mark 13:33). Each Believer should maintain an inwardly independent relationship in their earthly life, as to not be robbed of moral freedom, nor of their standing as a Christian in heart and lifestyle. He is not laying down rules, rather to not allow worldly relationships to fetter our standing with Christ, since *"this world in its present form is passing away"*.

11:26   The Lord's Supper is a solemn pledge of His coming again. Christ lived and died for all who will believe (John 3:16), and the Holy Supper is the link between the two comings of Christ; the memorial and monument to His First Advent for salvation, and the pledge of His return at His Second Coming for the completion of salvation and judgment on unsaved and rebellious humanity. The Supper has a backward and forward look, since it is to be observed *"until He comes"*.

15:20-26   Paul's great proclamation regarding the order of the resurrection. Christ was most assuredly *"raised from the dead"*, the *"first fruits"* of His sleeping people (Rev 1:5; Col 1:18). As death used here is physical death, so also by *"the resurrection of the dead"* is meant the resurrection of the body.

When Christ comes again, *"then they that are in Christ"* are resurrected, *"then cometh the end when He will deliver up the Kingdom to God"*. Paul is speaking throughout of the resurrection only of Believers.

"Each in his own order" - this means not so much priority, but rank, troop, division of an army. The Believers are conceived of as rising together, and the same will be for unbelievers. (1 Cor 15:50-52; 1 Thess 4:16, 17; 2 Thess 1:6-10; Matt 24:30, 31; Dan 7:13; 12:1, 2)

Next in order, but not necessarily immediately, comes *"the end"*; the end of the world as it is presently known, the end of all things, absolutely. Jesus will *"deliver up the Kingdom to God, the Father"*. Before this there must be an epoch of judgment before the end. The annulling of death will take place at the Great White Throne Judgment, after the Millennial Kingdom and final rebellion of Satan (Rev 20:7-15). Godet remarks, "The essential object of Christ's reign is the carrying out of this judgment on the opposing powers which still remain after His coming (Rev Chapter 20)."

"The last enemy to be destroyed is death." (Rev 20:14). Death has not been destroyed at the Second Coming and at the resurrection of those who belong to Christ. "It seems there is here taught two resurrections, the former for Believers only, the latter of all other people when at last death itself will die" - Principal Edwards. Other commentators are in agreement.

15:50-58   Paul reveals the *"mystery"*. *"We (Believers) will not all sleep, but we shall all be changed, in a moment, in the twinkling of an eye, at the last trumpet: for the trumpet will sound, the dead will be raised incorruptible, and we shall be changed."*

This *"change"* is from *"flesh and blood"*, the present physical human organism, into a glorified body suited to inherit the Kingdom, and to reign with Christ. *"We shall not all sleep, but we all (who are alive at the Parousia) shall be changed."* *"In a moment"* - literally, an "atom", a little indivisible point of time.

"At the last trumpet (sound)" - the divine signal by which the moment, and the event, will be proclaimed. The resurrection is instantaneous, not a long drawn out succession of stages. It seems the sound will be audible. It is, without doubt, the trump of God mentioned in 1 Thessalonians 4:16, and is the last trumpet of this age or dispensation. See commentary on Matthew 24:31.

In verse 54 Paul quotes from Isaiah 25:8. Death is to be completely conquered for Believers. (2 Cor 5:4) Verse 55 is a quote from Hosea 13:14, and Paul clarifies its meaning in verses 56 and 57. *"The sting of death is sin"* - it is sin that imparts to death its fatal power. Death is by sin. Sin is Satan's cause. See 5:5. (Rom 5:12)

"The power of sin is in the law" - because without law there would be no sin (Rom 4:15), because if there be no law there can be no condemnation (Rom 5:13). The law here is the law of God in its widest sense. (Gal 5:14; Rom 1:18-20; James 2:10)

1 Corinthians

"Victory through our Lord Jesus Christ" - victory over death because He has satisfied the demands of the law, and it has no power to condemn those who are clothed in His righteousness.
(Rom 8:1, 2; Eph 2:1-10)

Paul concludes his revealing of the *"mystery"* by encouraging Believers to not allow doubt, but to remain steadfast in the faith, and to perform the Christian life with its duties, especially that of bringing others to the knowledge of the Lord. This work will have its reward in the resurrection.
(Matt 28:18-20; Mark 16:15, 16; Luke 24:46, 47; James 5:20)

2 Corinthians   Written by the Apostle Paul.   About 57 AD

4:14   Christians may be conceived and designated as one day becoming raised with Jesus, since they are members of Christ. Christ is the first fruits of those raised from the dead.

5:1-10   Paul stresses the difference in outlook for the Believer relating to physical life and death. Death has no power or fear for the Believer as, *"we make it our aim...to be well pleasing to Him"*.

At the time of belief in Christ the Believer is *"given the Spirit as a deposit, guaranteeing what is to come"*. The Spirit gives confidence to *"live by faith, not by sight"*.

At the Believers death they pass immediately into glory.
(Matt 22:32; Phil 1:21-23; Heb 22-24; Luke 16:22)

At the judgment seat of Christ all must appear and *"receive what is due him for the things done while in the body, whether good or bad"*.

Moral actions are conceived here as something deposited, laid up, and which at the judgment are received back, carried away in earned reward and retribution.
(Acts 10:42; 17:31; Rom 2:16; 2 Tim 4:1; 1 Pet 4:5; Rev 20:4)

Ephesians   Written by the Apostle Paul.   62 AD

1:10   The present age (the dispensation) will be the fullness of times. The ordering of historical events, the arrangement beginning at the First Advent of Christ. The dispensation referred to is the Gospel dispensation inaugurated by that coming. It is an unknown period of time, season of time, strung out over centuries to be completed at an appointed time, at which *"to sum up all things in Christ...in the heavens...upon the earth"*.

2:7   *"The ages to come"* refers, without doubt, to the time of the Parousia. It is a looking forward to the ages of glory that follow the appearance of the Messiah.

4:30   *"The day of redemption"*, refers to the day when, at the Parousia, the certainty of deliverance into salvation becomes a reality, when the body is glorified with the Spirit; when the redemption shall be fully realized." - Meyer

5:5   The Kingdom of Christ and God is reserved for the pure in heart, not merely a future kingdom of glory, but the present kingdom of grace. (Matt Chapter 13)

5:27   The joyful presentation of the Church, holy and righteous. That this presentation is to take place at the Second Coming is generally admitted, the more so since this event is so frequently referred to as a marriage.

If *"a radiant Church"*, as here used, demonstrates the total number of those who will be saved, then as Dr. David Brown adduces this verse, together with Colossians 1:22, 23; 1 Thessalonians 3:13 and Jude verse 24, is proof that the Church will be absolutely complete at His coming, and that therefore there can be no conversion of the nations after that event. If this be so, the "rapture" must occur late, or at the end of the Great Tribulation. Many opponents of this interpretation call attention that it is nowhere declared in Scripture that this presentation of the Church to Himself takes place immediately upon His glorious appearing. (Rev 19:7; 21:2; 22:17)

He does gather the saints at His Second Coming, whenever that "rapture" event occurs. If the presentation of the Church is also the *"wedding of the Lamb"*, as noted in Revelation 19:7, then this must all occur at the end of the Tribulation and/or the beginning of the Millennium. It seems, within the context of Revelation 19, that this is the case.

Ephesians

In Revelation 21:2 and 22:17 is found the *"bride"* as a descriptive of the beauty of the new Jerusalem, and as a member of the blessed who participate in delivering the *"free gift"* of salvation message, *"the Spirit and the bride say, Come!"*. The invitation for salvation has a point when it is no longer presented, and no one is further saved. This point in time seems to be when the *"wrath of God"* is poured out on the unrepentant and ungodly during the Great Tribulation. (John 3:36; Rom 1:18; 2:8; Eph 5:6; Rev 6:17; 11:18; 14:19; 15:1; 19:15)

6:13   Paul offers a challenge, and encouragement, as the Believer struggles *"against the powers of this dark world and against the spiritual forces of evil in the heavenly realms"* (verse 12). "The whole passage seems to be concerned with a present struggle, but also a more specific day in which Satanic power puts forth its last and greatest outbreak, that is the last outbreak of the anti-Christian kingdom Paul expected shortly before the Parousia." - Meyer.

The *"heavenly realms"* most likely refers to the *"ruler of the kingdom of the air"* (Ephesians 2:2).
(See comments on Luke 21:34 - 36 and 2 Thessalonians 2:9-12)

Philippians   Written by the Apostle Paul.   60 AD

1:6-10   Paul praises *"the partnership in the Gospel"* by the Philippian Church (verse 5). His confidence is in Christ's ability to perfect their good work *"until the day of Jesus Christ"*, the day of His Second Coming. The *"day of Christ"* relates to the saint and his reward, rather than the sinner and his punishment.

There is in these verses a call to the Believer to grow in Christian maturity, to love and to grow in knowledge to *"discern what is best"*. (4:5-9) His call is to *"work out your salvation with fear and trembling"* (2:12) to *"not run in vain, nor labor in vain"* (2:16).

3:9-11   Paul's pedigree was of no account to put his confidence in *"the flesh"* (3:1-8). His justification for righteousness was *"through faith in Christ"*, to be *"found in Him"*, and to *"know Him"*. The *"power of His resurrection*" refers to the power which His resurrection exercises on the Believer in assuring them of their justification (Rom 4:25; 6:4; Col 2:12), and being raised with Him.

In verse 11 the possibility of failure is presumed. Paul knew that he would be resurrected. His use of *"resurrection from the dead"* is a debated expression. It can also mean *"from among the dead"*. No doubt Paul had in mind and referenced *"the blessed resurrection of the dead in Christ in which those who are Christ's shall rise at His Parousia"* (1 Cor 15:23; 1 Thess 4:16). The teaching of Scripture is that the Christian shall rise first (Rom 8:23; 1 Thess 4:16).

4:5, 6   The reference is to the Second Coming of Christ, concerning the immediateness of which there was an expectation at that time. "The Believer is to have a readiness to listen to reason, a yieldingness that does not retaliate. The motive for this sweet reasonableness is the soon return of Christ." - Wycliffe. The behavior of the Believer, especially in the end times, is to be bold in Christian witness without being obnoxious, ugly in attitude, and condemning, to not be a hostile witness to the unsaved. The Believer is to be known by "love". This does not mean acceptance of sinful and wrong behaviors.

In verse 6 Paul advises to control anxiousness and take everything in requests to God by prayer and petition. His focus is on those things that are worthy of putting into practice as a lifestyle for the Believer.

Colossians   Written By the Apostle Paul.   64 AD

1:13   This verse states the fact realized at the conversion of the Believer that the Kingdom is now present. The Believer has been rescued out of the kingdom of darkness into the kingdom of light, for redemption and the forgiveness of sins (verse 14) and freedom from human traditions and deceptive philosophies (2:8).

The Believer has not been rescued out from earthly trials and tribulations, as experienced in the lives of Believers for centuries, and carries on in these last days as Believers come under severe stress and tribulation. (1 Thess 1:10)

Colossians

3:4   At the Parousia of Christ, when He is no longer concealed from view, the Believers union with Him will also be manifested visibly in glory. The change occurs in a moment. (1 Cor 15:23)

1 Thessalonians   Written by the Apostle Paul.   51 AD
                             His earliest letter in the New Testament.

1:10   To wait for Christ's return *"who rescues us from the coming wrath"*, and to serve the living and true God (verse 9) are here set forth as the aim of conversion and the characteristic of the Christian life. God raised His Son from the dead and it is He who will rescue the Believer from God's wrath in the last days. Believers have not been "rescued" from man's wrath. (1 Thess 5:9)

It must be noted here that for centuries the Christian Believer has been stressed, killed, and persecuted by man. Look at the recent slaughter of Christians in the Middle East, especially Lebanon, in the latter part of the Twentieth Century, as one example. The Muslims killed thousands of Lebanese Christians, as the world stood by...

2:12, 13   Paul praises the Thessalonian Believers and encourages them to *"live lives worthy of God"*. He recognizes their belief in *"the Word of God"* that he had preached to them, apparently in great detail (2 Thess 2:5).

2:19, 20   Paul continues his excitement and joy in their steadfast belief, and the presence of the Lord at His coming will be a place of joy and glorying for them. This is the hope of the Believer who maintains the faith until death. (3:5, 12, 13; 2 Pet 1:10, 11; 2:20, 21; 3:14; Matt 13:18-21) Paul knew of the *"tempter"* that could possibly make his efforts with them *"useless"*. Satan snatches away the seed of faith, through temptations and deceit. (Matt 13:19)

3:12, 13   The Believer is to *"stand firm in the faith"*, to increase in grace, faith, and knowledge so as to be established, *"blameless and holy before God the Father at the coming of our Lord Jesus with all His saints (holy ones)"*. (Matt 13:23) This means either angels, glorified Believers, or both.

Alford says, "We need not enter into any discussion whether these are angels or saints properly so-called. The expression is an Old Testament one and was probably meant by Paul to include both. Certainly Jesus will be accompanied by the angels, but also with the Spirits of the just (Matt 25:31; 1 Thess 4:14; 2 Thess 1:7)."

Riggenbach says, "Saints are with Christ immediately after death and He will bring them with Himself, raising them before the rapture of the living, and thus they may be described as coming with Him."

4:13-18   Paul provides clarity about those who have died (fallen asleep) before the Second Coming of Jesus; the sequence of the rapture as the Believers blessed hope. No doubt the Thessalonian Believers were disturbed about their departed loved ones, and seem to have not been fully informed as to the first resurrection. (Rev 20:4, 5) Paul encourages them to not be ignorant and grieve as those who have no hope.

Why were they not to grieve? Because of belief in the resurrection of Jesus, and the fact that, *"those who have fallen asleep"* will come back with Jesus at His Second Coming. (John 5:28; 1 Cor 15:21)

It is very important to note that Paul provides the authority with which he writes this information; *"according to the Lord's own Word..."*. (verse 5). This is not an opinion or idea that Paul had - it is a special revelation directly from the Lord Himself given to the Apostle Paul.

In verse 16 it is very clear that the revelation of Christ at His Second Coming will be accomplished by Christ only, and none other. He comes with a call, a command, which reaches into the grave and awakens the sleeping Christian. They are summoned from their graves, responding to the trumpet call of God, the first to rise, then those Believers who are living are *"caught up as well to meet the Lord in the air"*. The *"caught up"* is a word which means *"snatched away"* by a swift and irresistible force. At the instant of this event the Believers will be changed. (1 Cor 15:51, 52)

Believers are *"caught up...in the clouds"*. The same idea is to be found in Psalm 104:3; Daniel 7:13; Acts 1:9-11; and Matthew 24:30. The Believers permanent abode with Christ is not in the air and clouds, but it is heaven. (2 Cor 5:1)

It is not clear if there is any period of time between this event and the return of Christ to reign.

1 Thessalonians

Olshaussen remarks that after Christ meets the saints He returns them to heaven, into His heavenly abode at the right hand of God, and that we read nowhere that Christ and the glorified Believers will reign on the earth during the Millennium. Paul says nothing about this here, one way or the other.

Revelation 20:9 makes this statement about events at the close of the Millennium; *"They* (Satan's Gog and Magog) *marched across the breadth of the earth and surrounded the camp of God's people, the city He loves."* This seems to indicate that some, or all, of *"God's people"* are on earth at this time, in Jerusalem, no doubt reigning over the earth then. Are they Jews, Christians, ones saved during the Millennium, or all saints of all time? Exactly who these are is not fully known.

5:1-6   The Believers will not be surprised at the sudden coming of the Day of the Lord. *"Times and seasons"* is the same expression used by Christ in Acts 1. *"Times"* denotes times in general, while *"seasons"* denotes definite points or periods of time. The expression used is not a haphazard one, as Campbell Morgan says, "It refers to the whole Providential arrangement marked out by God, and is here used with special bearing upon the time of the end when the Lord was to come again."

The exact time was unknown and could not be known; however, Believers are *"not in darkness"* as they watch and understand the *"day"* as described in Scripture.

The educated Believer has a Biblical worldview, and while not knowing *"the hour"*, yet has a definite knowledge of the period in contrast to the unbelieving world that knows not God and lives in slumber and ignorance, much as the condemned of Noah's day. (Gen 6:6, 7; Matt 24:38, 39)

Peter wrote in 2 peter 3:3, 4, *"scoffers will come"* and *"they will say, Where is this coming he promised?"*. This seems to indicate that there is to be a known expectation of His coming by Believers, and an awareness by the unbeliever that this expectation is long overdue, and to be ridiculed. Peter goes on to say, *"the Lord is not slow in keeping His promise...He is patient... wanting everyone to come to repentance"* (3:9). This indicates that there is a time when salvation is no longer available. (Amos 5:18-20)

Today many people in the world "know" of the expectation of His coming through television, movies and books. There is already much ridicule and "scoffing" at the belief in the return of Jesus.

The Moslems have their own version of a "messiah figure" that will return and bring a world wide conversion to Islam. There is at this time an effort for this Moslem "messiah" to appear.

Iranian President Mahmoud Ahmadinejad made an inflammatory speech to the U.N. General Assembly on Thursday, September 24, 2010. He began by praying, "O God, hasten the arrival of Imam al-Mahdi and grant him good health and victory and make us his followers and those who attest to his righteousness."

Imam al-Mahdi is another name for the "Twelfth Imam" or the "Hidden Imam." Shia Muslims believe this Islamic messiah will come at the End of Days to destroy Judeo-Christian civilization as we have known it, force infidels to convert or be executed, and will set up a one-world Islamic government known as the "caliphate."

Ahmadinejad believes the way to "hasten" the Twelfth Imam's coming is to annihilate the U.S. and Israel. This would bring about the "victory" that Ahmadinejad prayed for on American soil.

- From flashtrafficblog.wordpress.com (Joel Rosenberg)

Satan, as the great deceiver, is hard at work in the world today, as he knows his time is short. As *"sons of the day"* the Believer is *"not in darkness so that this day should surprise you like a thief"*. Keep your lamp lit! (Matt 25:1-13)

5:9   Paul goes on to challenge the Believer to be prepared for *"the day"* by *"putting on faith and love...the hope of salvation"*, for the Believer is not appointed to suffer the wrath of God.
(Isa 26:20; Dan 8:19; 11:36; 1 Thess 1:10)

5:19-23   Paul concludes his teaching and challenge to maintain a Christian lifestyle. In verses 19-22 Paul gives direct commands; *"Do not*

1 Thessalonians

put out (quench) the Spirit's fire, do not treat prophecies with contempt. Test everything...hold to the good...avoid every kind of evil."

At the Second Coming of Jesus the sanctified Believer is preserved, without blame. The Apostle seems here to teach the threefold division of human nature: the Spirit, soul, and body. The whole of man is to be *"kept blameless"*, preserved and brought together in *"the coming of our Lord Jesus Christ"*. (1 Cor 1:4-9)

2 Thessalonians   Written by the Apostle Paul.   52 AD

1:4-10   The church at Thessalonica was growing strong in the faith and enduring *"persecutions and afflictions"* as a result. It is only some months, perhaps a year or so, since Paul had written the first letter to them, and their growth brought sufferings that would result in *"being counted worthy of the Kingdom of God"*. The righteous judgment of God "is that which will be completed at the Lord's coming" - Alford.

Their present sufferings may be taken as a proof of the coming judgment upon their adversaries and the adversaries of God, because it is obvious that in this world persons do not receive their just deserts and therefore a future judgment is demanded for the sake of justice (verse 6).

In verse 7 is promised *"rest"* from earthly affliction and is one of the glories of the future kingdom, *"at the revelation of the Lord Jesus"*. The execution of the judgment at His coming will be *"in flaming fire"*, the natural symbol of perfect purity and unapproachable majesty, as well as *"blazing fire"*. The Lord's devastation of the earth is described in Isaiah Chapter 24.

In verse 8 is defined those who will receive punishment and be condemned: the unbelievers; and the willfully ignorant of God who obeyed not His Gospel that was preached to them. This most likely refers not only to those who openly reject the Gospel message, but also the apostate church, especially at the end time. Refer to comments on Romans 1:18, 19.

Verse 9 describes the punishment, *"everlasting destruction and shut out from the presence of the Lord..."*. This occurs *"on the day He comes to be glorified in His holy people and to be marveled at among all those who have believed"*. Olshausen says, "It is not stated here that Christ comes with His saints, as it was said in verse 7 that He comes with the angels, but according to 1 Thessalonians 4:17 (there gathering together with Him), this must here be necessarily assumed." There is no evidence in Scripture whether this passage referring to *"all"* is strictly limited to all those who have believed before the Second Advent.

2:1-13   There are many interpretation by noted scholars as to what is meant by Paul here in these verses in chapter 2. As these are studied the most clear distinction comes by understanding the plain and literal evidence of the words used, and how well they are verified by other Scriptures.

Paul begins here to clarify and expand on what he had earlier taught them regarding *"the day of the Lord"* (1 Thess 4:13-5:4). Here in verse 1 he states clearly that he is referring to *"the coming of our Lord Jesus Christ and our being gathered unto him..."*. There is no distinction between the *"coming"* in 1 Thessalonians and *"coming"* as used here. This is an important distinction for proper understanding.

Verse 2   Is a warning against false revelation, and falsely understood prophecies. Apparently Paul had been misquoted, misunderstood or purposefully attributed to some erroneous teachings, either orally, or by letter. The erroneous teaching was *"the day of the Lord had already come"*. They were confounded that Jesus Parousia had occurred and the persecutions they were experiencing put them in the times of the Tribulation.

Paul had taught them about the Second Coming of the Lord, both orally and in his first letter to them. They had obviously been deceived by the false report, supposedly from Paul. Here he sets out to correct their understanding.

Sir William Blackstone says, "The persecuted Thessalonians thought that they were in the Tribulation period, and that the day of the Lord had set in. But, Paul corrects them, first by reminding them that the Lord had not come for them yet, as He had said that He would (1 Thess 4:15-17). Paul then added things which must occur before the day of the Lord should come."

Verse 3   *"Don't let anyone deceive you in any way..."*. Paul gives a strong and specific warning here. "Beguile" and "befool" are in some

2 Thessalonians

ways a more accurate rendering, and carries the idea of deceit from evil intention. *"In any way"*, neither by any of the three ways mentioned in verse 2 (prophecy, report, or letter), or by any other method or way. Paul emphasizes the importance of this further information for their understanding of what is to be watched for before the Second Advent of Jesus.

Satan is known as the "great deceiver", and uses many methods to lead Believers astray from what is true. A little disinformation goes a long way in confusing the actual truth. Satan and his agents are masters at half-truth and deception. (Jude verses 4, 17) Paul is attempting to clarify here what must occur before the coming of Jesus for His saints. He is very plain spoken. (2 Pet 3:15, 16)

"For that day will not come until the rebellion (apostasy) occurs and the man of lawlessness (sin) is revealed."

Now it plainly seems that the Apostle Paul puts the *"rebellion (apostasy)"*, and the *"revealing of the man of lawlessness (sin)"* to be evident to the Believer before (*"that day will not come"*) the coming of Christ for His saints. If this be a true understanding then the Church cannot be raptured before these events. Further evident is that the *"man of sin"* (Antichrist) must be revealed, and when that revealing occurs it will be recognized by Believers and they will *"not be in darkness so that this day* (in context with 1 Thess 4:16, 17) *should surprise you like a thief"*. (1 Thess 5:4) The educated Believer is *"not in darkness"*.

The *"rebellion"*, or *"apostasy"*, or *"falling away"*, must also be active to be recognized by the Believer. The Thessalonians, due to the severe persecutions and sufferings they were experiencing (1:4) thought they were in Tribulation times.

Perhaps the *"false report"* was to blame for their confusion. Paul must have warned them in this regard, and it is evident by so many Scriptures that in the Great Tribulation times the Christian (and Jew) will come under the most severe stress and persecution.
(Matt 24:10-12, 22; Dan 7:19-22; Rev 7:14; 20:4)

"The falling away" - apostasy. This is preceded by the definite article *"the"*, and therefore refers to the apostasy as well known to the Thessalonians, either through oral instruction from Paul (Verse 5), or through Old

Testament prophecies, or the prophecy of Jesus in Matthew 24:9-12, which was written about 15 years before this letter from Paul.

Riggenbach says, "The falling away is the general rush of violent departure from the faith that precedes the final disclosure of the anti-Christian despot (1 Tim 4:1)." This departure from the faith must be caused by false teachers and the great persecutions and killings of Believers. (Rev 13:7, 17:1 - 6)

There are some modern commentators who translate this word *"apostasy"* as "departure", meaning a "spatial leaving or departure", as in the "rapture", rather than a "departure from the faith" as is referenced by so many other Scriptures.

This is a very weak meaning, and has been effectively refuted in a major scripture and word usage analysis by Dr. William Combs of the Detroit Baptist Seminary (DBSJ 3, Fall 1998: pages 63–87).

This "departure" must be from the faith and must be taken in the sense of a religious *"falling away"* as confirmed by constant Biblical usage in so many other Scriptures.

"The man of sin is revealed" - This man, a known personality, to be revealed in his time in such a way that there is no doubt that he is the Biblical Antichrist (verse 4). In past and present times numerous "candidates" have been variously identified as the Antichrist, but when he is *"revealed"* there will be no question in the mind of the educated Believer. (1 Thess 5:4)

Olshausen says, "The name 'man' characterizes him at the same time as a real man with body and soul, whom Satan, the prince of evil, makes his dwelling..." Even now the power of Antichrist is secretly at work, but at this future time will be revealed and will openly lead those who are perishing in every part of evil (verses 9, 10).

Verse 4   The character and desire of the *"man of sin"* is revealed, as he opposes *"against all that is called God"*. He is the Antichrist (1 John 2:18), the antagonist, the adversary, and caricature of Christ. He is not only against the true God, but against all forms of heathen gods as well. He treads all religions under his feet and sets himself up as the only object of adoration. (Dan 11:36, 37)
See comments on Daniel 7:8.

2 Thessalonians

"He will exalt himself...he sets himself up in God's temple", the temple in Jerusalem. "The fact that the temple no longer exists is not sufficient argument against the literal fulfillment...the temple is to be rebuilt...for this reason Ellicott leans strongly to an ultimate fulfillment in a future temple (Ezk 37:26) at Jerusalem." These comments were made long before Israel was reborn as a nation in 1948, and the current plans to rebuild the temple in Jerusalem. Reference Deuteronomy 28:64-68; Ezekiel 37:11-14; Isaiah 60:1-9.

It seems that Paul was here giving the most probable way by which the Believer would absolutely recognize and know for sure who the Antichrist is, and that the end was very near, and that the rapture of the Church was near at hand. (1 Thess 5:1-5) In this present day is clearly seen the worldly environment needed for these things to rapidly take place.

Verse 5   *"Don't you remember"* - Apparently Paul was telling them again what he had repeatedly talked to them about the coming of Christ, when he was with them.

Verse 6   Paul reminds them that they also *"know what is holding him back"*. That is, what hinders or restrains the appearance of the Antichrist until the time appointed for him by God. (Dan 11:27) Nowhere do we know, from Paul, what he says here about what they knew.

Verse 7   Continues the explanation about the mystery of the *"lawlessness"* (ungodliness, wickedness) as it corresponds with the rebellion (apostasy) of verse 3. It is already at work in their present time, in an as yet hidden, mysterious way. Paul sees the beginning of the final rebellion against final grace.

This rebellion against the ways of the Lord God Almighty will be a progressive rejection of what is revealed in the Holy Bible, and of those who believe, and their promotion of the God of the Bible, and His message therein. This rejection of all that is of God Almighty is strong in the world today.

What, who is *"the one...to be taken out of the way"*, that will unleash and release the final rebellion and the revelation of the Antichrist? There is very much debate and differences of opinion what, or who, is *"the one that restrains, or holds back"*.

Historically, the early Church took *"the restrainer"* as the government of the Roman Empire, the world power nation at that time, with its law and military power. Even the reformers of Martin Luther's time, who looked at the Pope, or Mohammed, as the Antichrist, said, *"the restrainer"* was the Roman Emperor. Some held that there was an eastern and western Antichrist, Mohammed and the Pope. The prevailing understanding was, *"the restrainer"* was the temporal political power of the time.

Wycliffe comments, "The Roman Empire has long since faded away...thus it seems probable that the restraining influence refers to the principle of human government manifest in the Roman State. Human institutions are part of God's program of common grace, whereby He bridles the forces of evil to provide the proper setting for the revelation of His special, redemptive grace. Totalitarian (rule) in the extreme (Rev 13:15-17), as Antichrist's government, is so diabolical (and anti-God) in nature that it utterly disqualifies itself for being considered a God-ordained human institution."

It must be noted that throughout history the totalitarian evil rulers and empires of the world have always been removed from power by other nations and governments. The restraining influence over "evil" governments and nations in more modern times has been seen as the early German Empire, the British Empire, or now the United States of America who is the primary world power and restrainer of evil in the Twentieth Century, and to the present time.

As yet the *"man of sin"* has not been revealed, and the apostasy, the lawlessness, the rebellion against God continues to manifest itself in a variety of ways. Ellicott says, "The restraining power of all well-ordered human rule, the principles of legality as opposed to those of lawlessness, of which the Roman Empire was the then embodiment (to keep the great outburst of godliness in check - 1 Peter 2:13; Titus 3:1)."

Others think that the restrainer is a person, the Holy Spirit indwelling the Believer in the Church. This is the position espoused by John Darby of the Plymouth Brethren in the early to mid 1800's, and of which Scofield became an advocate. It has become the dominant view of who *"the restrainer"* is in the pre-tribulation rapture theory position in many seminaries at the present time, and is taught in many of the Protestant churches today.

The implication of this position is that the Church must be removed before the *"lawless one - the man of sin"* can be revealed on earth. Therefore,

2 Thessalonians

the rapture of the Believer is to take place at the beginning of the Great Tribulation period of seven years. This is obviously a desired outcome, and one that people want to accept, since it means no severe persecutions and sufferings under the rule of the Antichrist.

The difficulty with the pre-tribulation rapture theory is the almost overwhelming whole Bible Scriptural evidence that indicates Believers being present during all, or a part of, the reign and rule of Antichrist. (Dan 7:21, 25; Matt 24:29-31; Rev 6:9-11; Luke 18:7, 8; 2 Thess 2:3)

In addition, Jesus plainly states in John 14:15, 16, 26, that the Holy Spirit will speak only of Him and will be the revealer of truth and of things to come. In Acts 1:7 the Holy Spirit is to give power to the Believer to be a witness for Jesus. Nowhere in Scripture is the role of the Holy Spirit to restrain evil, or the lawless one. The Holy Spirit is the convicter of sin, and the Counselor to the Believer (John 16:5-11). He seals Believers for the day of redemption (Ephesians 4:30).

Another very interesting idea regards *"the restrainer"* as the archangel Michael. He is depicted in Scripture as being the protector of Israel (Dan 12:1), and being of a restraining influence and function (Dan 10:13, 20, 21; Rev 12:7). Michael could be the one that is preventing a one-world government over which the Antichrist is one day to rule. When this restraining influence is removed, then the final events of the last days can begin. (2 Cor 10:3, 4; Eph 6:12; Psa 34:7; Acts 12:7-11; Dan 2:19 - 21, 44)

In Genesis 11:1-9, the Lord confused the language of men and scattered them all over the world as different nations. The reason God did this, according to Wycliffe, "is the men of that time defied God and set out to prove their self-sufficiency". Man continues to honor self and build towering structures to exalt themselves, and to spurn God's law and grace, just as these early men did.

As long as nations exercise their individual powers, there can be no unified world government or leader. The Antichrist person will be the one to finally put together a worldwide government that is able to control the world's commerce, economy and military power. It seems this one-world government and power will not be in harmony for long, as the various sectional "kings" will at some point rebel against the Antichrist leadership and go to war against him.

At this time in history there is an organization dedicated to fulfill this prophecy - the United Nations. See Addendum.
(Dan 8:15-27; Dan Chapter 11)

Verse 8   The revealed Antichrist is destined to be destroyed by the power and irresistible might of the reappearing Christ.

Verses 9-12   Here is described the *"work of Satan"*, the evil that deceives those who are perishing because *"they refused to love the truth and so be saved"*. They have *"delighted in wickedness"* and for this reason *"God sends them a powerful delusion"*. They have *"believed the lie"*, rather than the truth of the Gospel.
(Rom 1:18-23; 2:8-11)

In Paul's concluding remarks to the Believers at Thessalonica he challenges them to *"hold to the teachings we passed on to you"*, and warned them *"to keep away from every brother who is idle, and does not live according to the teachings you have received from us"* (3:6).

This is a strong command. In 3:14, 15 Paul further instructs the Believers who obey his teachings to not associate with those who do not; and to *"not regard him as an enemy, but to warn him as a brother"*.

A primary purpose of this commentary is to "warn the brothers and sisters in Christ" to Be Not Deceived, and to study the Scriptures diligently so as to be an effective witness in these last days, and to be prepared to live as a steadfast Believer during the reign of the Antichrist for some period of time, if that is indeed required of the Believer, as many Scriptures indicate.

Of equal importance is to reveal the mercy and saving grace of God through His Son Jesus, the Christ, the Messiah, to those who are perishing in unbelief, and who are deceived by the lies and works of Satan. See information at Acts 2:29-36.

1 Timothy   Written by the Apostle Paul.   62 AD

4:1   Paul gives specific instructions to Timothy about the apostasy *"in later times"*, and to teach these things *"to the brothers"*.

This is the only place in Scripture where the Holy Spirit is said to have spoken *"expressly"* or *"clearly"*, a direct prophecy by the Spirit to Paul himself. It should be viewed as pointing to the last times in the future immediately preceding the Second Coming of Christ. (2 Thess 2:3)

"Some will abandon the faith and follow deceiving spirits." The faith in the Gospel of Christ as revealed in the Scriptures, and no doubt a great many will be deceived, persecuted, and diverted from the true faith into a false Satanic influenced seducement to believe a lie. Refer to comments on Matthew 24:10-12.
(2 Tim 3:5, 7; Heb 3:12-15; 2 Pet 2:1-3; 3:3, 4)

6:14, 15   Paul charges Timothy to remain faithful in all that Christ has commanded, the rule of the Gospel, the Gospel viewed as the rule of life. (John 12:44-50) By keeping the Gospel in faith it will not be open to reproach or stained by sinful actions.

The keeping of this commandment is to be *"until the appearing"*. The Greek for this last word is "epiphany", meaning "appearing or brightness".

This passage shows that it is God who will bring to pass the epiphany of Jesus Christ, and will do so in His own time.
(Titus 1:3; Gal 4:4; 1 Tim 2:6; Acts 1:7)

2 Timothy   Written by the Apostle Paul.   67 AD

According to Wycliffe this second letter to Timothy contains the last words found in the Bible written by Paul. He wrote this letter from prison shortly before his martyrdom.

1:9-12, 18   Paul expresses his confidence in the security he has in the day of his Lord's coming. Jesus first appearing (epiphany) *"abolished death and brought life and immortality to light through the Gospel"*.

Paul was personally chosen to be the Gospel preacher to the Gentiles, and as such *"knows Him whom I have believed..."*. Paul experienced the proofs of Jesus through divine revelations. He committed his life to proclamation of the Gospel. He had entrusted himself, body, soul and spirit, into the keeping of his heavenly Father, and lay safe in His hands, confident in his future care at the coming of Christ again.

2:12   When the Messianic Kingdom is established, the enduring Believer shall reign with Christ, after the Parousia. (Rom 5:17; 8:17; Rev 20:4)

3:1, 9 , 13   The last days are to be times of great distress. It is agreed by practically all scholars that, *"in the last days"* refers to the time immediately preceding the Second Coming of Christ.

In verses 1-5 Paul provides the characteristics of the self-centered godlessness of people in general. In verse 13 this godlessness progressively gets *"worse and worse"*, prompted by evil *"deceivers and impostors"*.

Here is seen the leading astray by deception, as well as deception through the practice of magic arts, or "incantations by howling", which is a meaning of "impostors". To the educated Believer (3:16, 17) their *"folly will be clear to everyone"*.

4:1, 3   *"Christ Jesus, who shall judge the living and the dead."* It is the physically living and the physically dead who are to be judged at the time in question, not some spiritual meaning. This is related to the appearing, the coming of Christ and His Kingdom which begins with the return of the Lord. The time of the judgment is not clear. Some think after the Millennium and some at the beginning, or perhaps both.

In verse 3 is found a description of the apostasy of the Church in the last days. They will find *"sound doctrine"* intolerable because it is not consistent with their desires. Their desire is to hear something *"tickling"* to their ear. They will surround themselves with teachers that cater to their own willful selfish desires instead of obedience under the divine will. The plain teachings of Scripture are cast aside.

It is a sad note that many churches today have moved from preaching and teaching the pure word of the truth of the Scriptures, and have liberalized

2 Timothy

the Gospel of Jesus to accommodate the current values, desires and culture of the people.
(Matt 24:10-12; Mark 8:28)

4:7, 8   Paul sees the end of his earthly struggle coming to a close. He has done all he could to proclaim the Truth of the Gospel, he has *"kept the faith"*. (2 Thess 1:11) Laid up for him *"the crown of righteousness"* - the crown which is bestowed as a recognition of righteousness and rewards the righteous course of life in Christ, who makes the award. All who do likewise will also be so awarded.

Paul seemed under no allusion that, *"keeping the faith"* was to be an endurance, a lifetime effort and activity, believing in the Lord.
(James 1:12; 1 Pet 5:4; Rev 2:10)

4:17, 18   Paul gives the reason for his assurance; *"the Lord stood at my side, and gave me strength."* This enabled him to fulfill his life's purpose of proclaiming the Gospel message to the Gentiles. *"Every evil work"* refers to the attacks suffered by evil temptations.

"Heavenly kingdom" refers to the threefold aspect of the kingdom, and Paul is familiar with them all. Colossians 1:13 says Christians are already translated into the kingdom of His dear Son; Philippians 1:23 anticipates for Believers immediately after death an entrance into the heavenly kingdom in which there is a fuller fellowship with Christ than any earthly experience can provide.

The primary conclusion from these verses may be summed up as follows from Wycliffe, "Paul was delivered out of the mouth of the lion (Philippians) and resumed his work so that the preaching might be fully known. Now, however, in the face of imminent death Paul was confident of the ultimate victory - not that he would escape death, but that God would keep him faithful *"unto His heavenly kingdom"*.

| **Titus** | Written by the Apostle Paul. | 62 AD |

2:13   The Believer's *"blessed hope"* is looked for, is expected. *"Hope"* is the thing hoped for, something definite and substantial. This is a hope that brings the blessedness for the Believer at the glorious appearing. The *"appearing"* (epiphany) emphasizes the visibility of the Second Coming. (Acts 2:11)

"Of our great God and Savior Jesus Christ" - Ellicott says, "It does indeed seem difficult to resist the conviction that our blessed Lord is here said to be our great God, and that this text is a direct, definite and even studied declaration of the Divinity of the eternal Son."
2 Peter 1:2 makes the same thought.

Hebrews   Writer unknown, various opinions.   About 64 AD

1:2, 8   The superiority of Jesus, the Son, over the prophets of old is proclaimed, *"at the end of these days"*, refers to the last days, the times of the Messiah. *"These days"* means the days in which they were now living belong to *"the end of days"*. The throne of God (Christ) will be established unto eternity and means that the dominion of Christ is to endure forever.

3:7, 8, 15; 4:7, 8 There are a number of instances in Scripture which the word *"day"* is used to express a greater period of time than twenty-four hours. It can mean a period of time.

"For the Church it is the whole time until Christ's Second Coming. For the Believer it is the period of his life." - Westcott.

8:7-13   The old covenant is being replaced by the new covenant in Christ. The old covenant's purpose had been thwarted by the fault of those who received it, not the covenant law itself. Their unfaithfulness did not annul the faithfulness of God, as proved by establishing the new covenant. Verse 10 declares this new covenant to be with the *"house of Israel"* and refers to the whole nation, and to the people of God in general. Verse 11 states the knowledge of the Lord would be widely spread in the Church, the people being brought by the Holy Spirit into true fellowship with God.

The new covenant rests upon forgiveness on the part of God, and not by performance on the part of man, as did the old covenant. *"He has made the first one obsolete; and what is obsolete and aging will soon disappear."* As yet this prophecy has received only partial fulfillment. Its complete fulfillment

Hebrews

comes when *"the knowledge of the Lord shall cover the earth as the waters cover the sea".*
(Jer 31:31-34; Joel 2:28, 29; Isa 54:13; Matt 11:11; Luke 7:28; John 6:45; 1 John 2:20, 27)

9:25-28   Christ's sacrificial death on the cross was offered only once, as a presentation of Himself with His blood before God in the heavenly Holy of Holies. He entered once for all, without need for renewal as was required under the old covenant by the High Priest. (Rom 6:10)

The *"end of the ages"* marks a point of termination of a series of preparatory ages, the ages being pre-Messianic and covering the whole period indicated by *"since the foundation of the world".* Jesus first came *"to bear the sins of many"* (Isa 53:12) and will *"appear a second time"* at His Parousia, not as a sin bearer, but as the judge.

His Second Coming is to consummate salvation *"to them that wait for Him".* Patient endurance and looking is called for. (10:37)

10:12, 13   Christ now sits at the right hand of God, patiently awaiting the day of His Parousia when He subdues His enemies. Paul gives the "order" of subduing in 1 Corinthians 15:23-26.

10:25   The Lord's return should be incentive for worship and *"exhorting one another"* to fidelity and good works. Considering the time that this was written, just as the war that lead to the Destruction of Jerusalem was beginning, the thought that the Parousia of Christ to be not far away is too clearly revealed to be denied.

The approaching judgment on Jerusalem and the Jewish people (Luke 21:5-36) of which so many signs were appearing, brought home the thought of His coming. So it is also today, as is seen the appearance of so many prophetic signs that His Second Coming is very near, especially the "sign" of Israel as a nation on "the land" promised to them by God.

10:37   The coming One, Jesus, since His ascension He has always been coming, His return being a matter of constant expectation. The signs given in Scripture of His return will be looked for, and seen by His educated and not deceived Believers. (Heb 10:25; 1 Thess 5:4)

12:22-27   The writer of Hebrews speaks of the end of the present age, and the promise to the Believer that Jesus is qualified as mediator of the new covenant presented. The old earth and heavens will be giving away to the new, accomplished by great physical convulsions with which a new heavens and new earth are to emerge out of the ruin of the old.

"Made in order that they may await the unshakeable things" - indicates that when the material present world has served its purpose, it will be removed and changed into God's heavenly city and eternal Kingdom, so that the things *"unshakeable"* will abide forever. (Rev 21:1-8)

James   Written by James, Jesus brother.   About 60 AD

5:3, 7-9   These are the only four verses in the whole epistle of James devoted to the subject of the Second Coming of Jesus. He gives exhortations to the *"brethren"* for *"patience until the coming of the Lord"*. They are encouraged to be steadfast and to stand firm, to confirm and strengthen their faith. (Luke 18:1-8)

In addition they were to not *"murmur"* or *"grumble"* against one another, a type of sinful irritability that could bring judgment that violates the Lord's injunction in Matthew 7:1-5.

1 Peter   Written by the Apostle Peter.   64 AD

The storm clouds were gathering preceding the Jewish war with the Romans that began in 66 AD. It is only six years before the Destruction of Jerusalem. No doubt Peter and the others were apprehensive about the current events of their day, and hoped for Jesus soon return.

1:3-7   It is the *"power of God"* in the Believers faith that guards the salvation promised and to be revealed when Christ shall be revealed *"in the last time"*. Fausset says, "The last time is the last day, closing the day of grace; the day of judgment, of redemption, of the restitution of all things, and of perdition of the ungodly." It is referred to in Matthew 13:39-43 as *"the end of the age"*.

1 Peter

Campbell Morgan says, "The hope of the Church is, in this aspect, a salvation to be revealed in all it's fullness when Jesus Christ Himself shall come." (Rom 8:19; 1 John 3:2)

1:13, 20   Peter says to be holy, to *"set your hope fully on the grace to be given you when Jesus Christ is revealed"*. Jesus was *"chosen before the creation of the world"*. His revealing is *"in these last times for your sake"*.

4:5, 7, 13   As the Believer anticipates the return of Christ, this should be inspiration to a sober minded and patient endurance. The judgment is standing ready; a time of preparedness, patience, joy and reward for Believers, and a time of God's wrath, terror and destruction for the ungodly. (2 Tim 4:1)

5:1, 4   Believers shall be partakers in *"the glory that shall be revealed"* at the time of the visible return of the Lord. It is a permanent *"crown of glory"*!

2 Peter   Likely written by the Apostle Peter.   67 AD

1:10, 11   Peter exhorts the Believers to be *"eager to make your calling and election sure...to never fall"*. According to Wycliffe the idea here "is the personal responsibility with reference to God's call and choice of the Believer, to keep on doing the faith so as to not stumble." (2 Pet 3:17) As a result of a sure faith the reward is *"entrance (a rich welcome) into the eternal Kingdom of our Lord and Savior Jesus Christ"*.

1:16-21   *"We did not follow cunningly devised fables"*.
Peter, and the other disciples, were eyewitnesses to the life, teachings, miracles performed, transfiguration glory, resurrection from the dead of Jesus, and His ascension up into the cloud. The authenticity of their witness reinforces the reality of *"the power and coming of our Lord Jesus Christ"*. The whole treasure of divine power is centered in Him (Matt 28:18). The coming here is His Presence, both at His First Advent and especially His future Second Coming in Glory.

In verses 19-21 is an amazing assessment of the validity of the Old Testament Scriptures. "Peter declares them to be more dependable than a voice from heaven heard with the natural ear" - Wycliffe.

Jesus took the Old Testament Scriptures as true, valid and literal, as did the Apostles. So then, we also should in this present age accept and apply the ancient Old Testament prophecies as valid, literal, and to be fulfilled. As Peter wrote in verse 19, *"You will do well to pay attention to it* (the word of the prophets)*".* (2 Pet 3:2)

Chapter 2   Contains warnings against the inevitability of false teachers, and the judgment of false teachers.

2:1   *"They will be among you and introduce destructive heresies, denying the Lord...".* This apostasy in the church and among the members has eternal consequence (verses 20 - 22).

2:2   *"Many will follow their shameful ways and bring the way of truth into dispute."*

2:3   *"These teachers will be greedy and make up stories..."*

2:4-12   Examples are given about God's judgments in the past on false prophets and rebellious angels and ungodly people, along with God's provision of rescue for the righteous from judgment. There is here a condemnation of the arrogance of the sinful nature of these teachers, who are *"like brute beasts, creatures of instinct born only to be caught and destroyed, and like beasts they, too, will perish."* (Col 2:6-18)

2:13-19   Further descriptions of the ungodly behaviors of these people, their depravity and their being *"a slave to whatever has mastered them".* (Rom 1:18-32)

2:20-22   Wycliffe says of these controversial verses, "This is a solemn assessment of the awful responsibility of apostasy, and it constitutes an implicit warning to Believers to remain steadfast." See commentary on Matthew 13:47-50; Mark 8:38; Luke 18:1-8.

3:3-10   The *"last of the days"* is the *"day of the Lord".* Not a single day, but those immediately preceding the Second Coming of Christ. Since the delay of His coming has now been so long this brings out the self-will and opposition (apostasy) to the will of God.

2 Peter

People are openly challenging the truth of God's Word spoken through the *"holy prophets"* - verse 2. These *"mockers"* want to know *"where is the promise of His coming?"*.

They openly ridicule belief. This shows that the Gospel is familiar among most everybody, as it is today.

Indicated is a strong and willful ignorance and unbelief of the plain teachings of Scripture. In verses 5-7 Peter reminds the reader that, *"by the Word of God"* (John 1:1-5) the origins of the earth came into existence, and at one time the world was judged and then destroyed by water. The next judgment will be by *"fire, being kept for the day of judgment and destruction of ungodly men"*. (Isa 24:6)

In verses 8-10 is declared the reality of how God sees time. Our understanding of a day is limited by astronomical event. His *"day"* is unlimited, as He may ordain time in a different manner. An example of this may be found in Daniels vision of the Seventy Weeks, which by historical reckoning are weeks of years.

The conclusion of the *"Day of the Lord"* is reiterated here by Peter to show the *"scoffers"* that He will come and execute His will in spite of any seeming delay. This will occur at God's appointed time, not man's. (Dan 11:27, 35, 36)

3:11-18   Peter's solemn declaration about the coming destruction of the world lead to this challenging question: *"What kind (manner) of people ought you to be?"* His answer is straight to the point: *"You ought to live holy and godly lives as you look forward to the day of God and speed its coming."* The idea is that of accelerating the arrival of that day by our holy lives and our labors for the Gospel. (James 1:4; Acts 20:24; Luke 21:24; Rom 11:25)

In verses 14-18 Peter advises the Believer with a repeated urging to be diligent and make it your business to be educated and spiritually literate. He sites the difficult to understand writings of Paul as authoritative and places them with other sacred Scriptures. *"Be on your guard"* - do not be deceived and lead astray, but *"grow in the grace and knowledge of our Lord and Savior Jesus Christ"*.

1 John   Written by the Apostle John.   90 AD

2:18, 22, 28   The great Jewish/Roman war and Destruction of Jerusalem occurred about 20 years prior. John says, *"it is the last hour"*. He has here in mind the last period of this world, and the coming of Christ Jesus. He introduces the term *"antichrist"*, which means "against Christ, instead of Christ, or a false Christ". It is in a sense "antagonistic to Christ".

These antichrists in John's time were the heretical teachers who had gone out from the Church (verse 19), who were clothed with the attributes, had the spirit of, and were the forerunners of the personal coming Antichrist. This is the same enemy that Paul speaks of in 2 Thessalonians 2:3, 4. It is the enemy that is becoming more dominant in the world on this very day.

In verse 22 John defines the character of the Antichrist by asking, *"Who is the liar?"*. The answer is defining; *"It is the man that denies that Jesus is the Christ...he denies the Father and the Son."*

This is the anti-Christian principle, to deny Jesus is the Christ is to also deny the Father and the Son as well. Look carefully at those of this present time who so aptly fit this description.

Verse 28 is a challenge to *"continue in Him"*. This is a command to keep His commandments and teachings, to be *"confident and unashamed before Him at His coming"*. "The Believer is to be doing what is good and right, being steadfast in the faith, as when He comes we shall give an account of our stewardship to Him."- Wycliffe. (1 Thess 3:13; 5:23; James 5:7, 8)

3:2, 3   As Believers there will come a moment, *"in the twinkling of an eye"*, that we shall be changed by the power of God and have our first view of the risen Jesus in His Glory. We shall be like Him because we shall see Him face to face!
(2 Cor 3:18; Job 19:25, 26)

4:2, 3   The spirit of the antichrist is already in the world. The Spirit of God, the Holy Spirit, the indwelling of the Believer is proved by confessing *"that Jesus Christ has come in the flesh from God"*.

1 John

Oral confession with the mouth is meant. The spirit of antichrist denotes not only denial, but contradiction as well. This evil spirit speaks from the viewpoint of the world and the world listens to them (verse 5).
(2 John 7, 8)

Jude   Written by Jude, brother of Jesus.   66 AD

Verses 3, 4   Believers are urged to *"contend for the faith"*, as *"godless men"* had *"slipped in among you"*. False teachers were in the Church early, and now present in the modern Church as apostates of the Gospel. The Biblically educated Believer is not fooled.
(2 Thess 2:1-3; 2 Pet 3:14-18)

Verse 6   Fallen angels left their assigned habitation and as a result have been placed in captivity until *"judgment on the great day"*. There are several views on this proclamation.

A vague reference to Genesis 6:1-7, about angels marriage to descendants of Cain, and that this sin refers to the revolt of Satan and his angels. Jude may have gotten this information from the book of Enoch. (1 John 3:3; 1 Pet 3:19, 20; Rev 12:7-9)

Verses 14-21   Judgment pronounced upon all the ungodly activities and words of persons, the *"mockers"* of God, and upon apostate teachers. *"Enoch, the seventh from Adam"* is significant as to Adam was given the first promise of the Lord as Savior, and to Enoch was given the first promise of His Second Advent as judge. This judgment is *"in the last time"*.
(2 Pet 3:3-10)

Verse 24   The glory that shall be revealed when Jesus Christ comes for the Believer, who has not *"stumbled"*, but through faith has been guarded and kept from falling. The joyful presentation of the Church is complete, without blemish, prepared for the marriage supper of the Lamb.
(Eph 5:25-27; Col 1:22-25; 1 Thess 3:13; 5:19-24; Heb 9:15, 28; Rev 19:6-9)

The Book of Enoch
(Considered by most Bible scholars a pseudoepigraphal work.)

According to the biblical narrative (Genesis 5:21-24), Enoch lived only 365 years, a short life compared to the other patriarchs before the Flood. Enoch "walked with God; then he was no more for God took him."

Although the original version was lost in antiquity, the discovery of the texts as part of the Dead Sea Scrolls, from Qumran Cave 4 in 1947, has finally provided parts of the Aramaic original.

Though it was once believed to be post-Christian (the similarities to Christian terminology and teaching are striking). Discoveries of copies of the book among the Dead Sea Scrolls prove that the book was in existence before the time of Jesus Christ. The date of the original writing upon which the second century B.C. Qumran copies were based is shrouded in obscurity. It is, in a word, old. Jesus and the Disciples were probably familiar with the writings.

Revelation   Written by the Apostle John.   96 AD

Introduction

This introduction gleaned from The Wycliffe Bible Commentary, with additional comments by the author.

The book of Revelation is the most difficult in the Bible. It's content and the understanding of it are inexhaustible. To even begin to make sense of these difficult chapters requires a certain fundamental understanding of some principles of interpretation. (See the beginning of Chapter 6)

In spite of these difficulties, this book is the necessary conclusion to God's revelation to humanity, and as such is worthy of careful study (Rev 1:3), as this is the prophetic book of the end of this present age, and the start of the next.

It presents a time of terrible upheaval, fearful events and the final rebellion of the ungodly, lead by Satan. The unleashing of these vast powers of evil bring about a one world condition. This whole world is deceived into a one world government that has authority over all the nations for a time. It is the most perilous of all known times.

Revelations is a book of visions, and is saturated with symbolic language. In these symbols is found the completeness, the perfection, the fullness of God's dealing with His creation. The number seven is dominate, and is considered the number of completeness and perfection. Note how many occurrences of the number "seven" are found in Revelation. A separate study of numbers as used in the Bible is a worthy endeavor.

The relationship of Revelation to Daniel, the Olivet discourse by Jesus, and much of the prophetic Scriptures is undeniable. The consistency of the message declares a common author; the Lord God Almighty, Himself.

1:1-10   *"The Revelation of Jesus Christ..."*. The revealing, the coming of the Lord, is the theme. Jesus is the author and the subject. It is made to all of Christ's servants, through the Apostle John, either from Christ Jesus Himself, or an angel on His behalf. The events revealed will come to pass *"before long"*. (Rev 22:7) We are told to wait patiently, as there are successions of many intermediate events which must first elapse (13:10; 14:12).

In verses 7 and 8 is seen the theme of the Apocalypse. Jesus return is visible to all peoples of the earth (Dan 7:13, 14; Matt 26:64; Acts 1:9-11). It is a coming to judgment, as *"all the peoples of the earth will mourn because of Him"*. This is the fulfillment of Zechariah 12:10, as well as an allusion to Matthew 24:30, which puts the mourning *"immediately after the tribulation days"*. It seems the Church may have been *"caught away"* before this event, as the Believers attitude would not be one of *"mourning"*, but one of relief and joy. It may be the two events; "rapture" and Second Coming, are nearly simultaneous. (Matt 24:29-31)

1:19   Here is given the threefold natural division of the Book of Revelation:

"The things you have seen" - the visions shown to John.

"The things that are now" - the state of things in the seven mentioned churches when John was writing (Chapters 2 and 3), and/or portraying the course of the Church from John's time to the end of the present age, the time of the Second Advent.

"The things that will take place later" - the things symbolically represented in Chapters 4 - 22. These *"things"* also seem to represent literal events that are to occur during the last days and in the Great Tribulation period, the Millennium, and including the establishment of *"a new heaven and a new earth"*.

2:25-28   The ones who maintain the faith are to *"hold fast until I come"*. (Jude verse 3) Then they will be given *"authority over the nations"*. This refers to the authority conferred on the saints when they shall inherit the earth and reign with Christ in His Kingdom, as He shepherds the nations *"with a rod of iron"*. Most likely this refers to the Millennium period.

"The Morning Star" most likely refers to the heavenly glory of the victorious Christ Himself. (Dan 12:3; Matt 13:42; 1 Cor 15:40)

3:10-12   The patient endurance of the faithful Believer will result in being kept *"from the hour of trial"*. The precise meaning of *"keep you from"* is not clear. It could mean "out of" or "out from among" the dead.

Revelation

"The hour of trial" most likely refers to the time of the Great Tribulation. (Matt 24:21; 1 Pet 4:12) This is the well known *"hour"*.

The various ideas on the time of the rapture of the faithful Church comes into view here. The idea of exemption, or being taken away from, may support the pre-tribulation catching up of the Church.

If the faithful Church is not "caught up" until after the Great Tribulation, and goes through all or part of this period, then the meaning is *"to deliver out of"*, in the sense of bringing safely through the trials (John 17:15). An example of *"being delivered out of"* is when the Israelites were kept from the plagues on Egypt, in whose midst they were present.

Another idea is a period of severe persecution of the true Church before the Great Tribulation. This idea is difficult to verify. If this be so then the revealing of Antichrist must occur also, as he is given power that, *"wears out the saints"* (Dan 7:21; 8:23-25). It seems the positive revealing of the Antichrist comes at the beginning of the Great Tribulation period, or near the midpoint (Dan 7:25; 2 Thess 2:3), while the Church is still present on earth.

During this period all people on earth will be *"tested"*. The Believer is told to *"hold on to what you have so that no one will take your crown"*. No doubt this must refer to *"testing"*, and the Believer is to maintain the faith and not deny the Gospel.

This need to *"hold fast, hold on, be steadfast, etc.",* is a constant theme of Scripture. In every letter to the Revelation churches there is the admonition to *"overcome"*. The overcomer's are promised a place, forever, in the *"new Jerusalem"* (verse 12). Believers have been required to be "overcomer's" ever since. There are many Christian martyrs.

4:1-11   John is here taken up into heaven, *"in the spirit"*. No where is it indicated John went bodily into heaven, but rather in a trance or ecstasy. He was shown *"things which must come to pass hereafter"*. Later, after this, in the future.

Some use this *"taking up"* of John as reference to the rapture of the Church. "This cannot be approved by any accepted method of interpretation, and must be convicted of error." - Alford.

John was given an astounding vision of *"a throne in heaven with someone sitting on it"*. The detailed description of this visual experience may be part real, part symbolic. There are many ideas about what the items presented may mean. Suffice it to say verse 11 calls attention to the reverence, humility and recognition due to Him who sits on the throne. He is the Creator of all things!

5:1-14   John's vision continues as he sees a sealed book in the hand of Him that is on the throne. *"Who is worthy to open the book?"* One of the elders around the throne answers, *"The Lion that is of the tribe of Judah, the root of David, hath overcome to open the book and the seven seals thereof."*

No doubt this refers to Jesus Christ, due to His absolute victory over the power of darkness and sin and death. (Rev 22:16)

The contents of the sealed book have various interpretations, and the most acceptable referred to is the Apocalypse, which deals with what is to follow; Chapter 6 and the following chapters to the end of the Revelation.

The *"worthiness of the Lamb"* is recognized and praised by song, music and the prayers of the saints. The throne was encircled by an enormous throng of angels who sang with a loud voice, *"Worthy is the Lamb who was slain, to receive power and wealth and wisdom and strength and honor and glory and praise!"* All creatures *"in heaven and on the earth and under the earth, and on the sea, and all that is in them, singing..."*. This scene John saw was beyond magnificent and the adoration given to the Lamb was loudly and enthusiastically proclaimed for all to hear.

A brief review of the four Systems of Interpretation of the Book of Revelation.

1. The Spiritual System claims the book deals only with great principles and is a poetic and prophetic depiction of the struggle between good and evil; Christ and Satan. This is contradictory to the claims within the book and is altogether inadequate.

2. The Preterist System holds that the Revelation has largely been fulfilled, mostly by events in John's own time by the Destruction of Jerusalem and subsequent events of the first century. It has few supporters at this time, as it is generally conceded that Revelation was not written until 96 AD, some twenty-six years after that event.

Revelation

3. <u>The Historical System</u> holds that the prophecies of Revelation embrace the whole history of the Church and its foes, from the time of writing to the end of the world. As a system of interpretation many scholars think it quite too incomplete. Much of the whole school of historical interpretation has been irretrievably discredited.

4. <u>The Futurist System</u> throws the whole book, beginning with Chapter 4, forward to the times of the Second Coming of Christ. This view has three primary aspects to be considered.

   One, which puts all the happenings after the rapture of the faithful Church, and during the Great Tribulation;

   Another which places the Believer on earth during the Great Tribulation, to be raptured at the end, just before the Millennium;

   And another which understands that the Believer will be raptured prior to the "wrath of God" being poured out on the earth, at, or after the midpoint of the Great Tribulation, or near the end of the Tribulation events. These all fit within the pre-millennial rapture of the faithful Church position. This Futurist view gives to literal Israel a very large place in the book.

There are deep mysteries in these prophetic Scriptures. The following brief summaries of Chapters 6 - 22 are not at all conclusive or exhaustive in study. The serious student will want to dig deeper, and there are many fine scholarly works that present a variety of interpretations for consideration.

Keep in mind that whatever idea is considered it must be verified by other Scriptures and fit within the overall context of the events being studied. As noted on numerous occasions in Scripture, the Believer is warned about being deceived and mislead.

Satan and his agents are masters at being able to confuse, deceive and discredit the plain teachings of Scripture. Mix error with truth and the deception is effective. (In my personal experience as a visitor I heard, from a pulpit in a major denomination church, a minister say much of the Old Testament was a "Jewish myth". He was not challenged.)

Furthermore, as Believers see current events in the world focus on the small nation of Israel, the city of Jerusalem and the Jewish peoples, plus the rapid development of a one-world governmental, economic and religious system, we know that the present age is nearing its end, and the Second Coming of Jesus Christ must be at hand. There will be a continuing unfolding of prophecy fulfillments and understanding until Jesus returns.

Chapter 6   The Six Seals.

6:1, 2   The First Seal. John continues relating what he is seeing, as the first seal is opened by the Lamb. Roman victors always rode on white horses and it seems here to be the image of a victorious warrior going forth to conquer. Who is this rider? There are many opinions. A personification of the Antichrist going forth, proclaiming false peace and establishing a one-world government of nations seems to fit. (Dan 7; Matt 24:5-14)

6:3, 4   The Second Seal. *"A red horse"* is war personified. The color of the horse in each case has reference to the function of the rider, and in this case it is to *"take peace from the earth"*. The false peace of the Antichrist gives way to his waging war against those nations (kings) who oppose him. (Dan 7:11; Ezk 38, 39)

6:5, 6   The Third Seal. Black being the color of hunger, the riders purpose is to bring famine and scarcity on the earth. Apparently the availability of food will be such that its cost will be very high. The *"red horse"* brought war, and war brings disruption to the supply of food, and its distribution.

Today the world's food supply consists of produce from many countries being distributed over a large geography by air, land and sea. War, combined with unseasonable weather and distribution difficulties, would immediately cause great shortages and distress in the food chain of the world.

6:7, 8   The Fourth Seal. *"A pale horse"*, the color here is that of a corpse, the pallor of death. The rider is named *"Death"*. Death has a companion, *"Hades"*. Both are here personified and have authority over *"the fourth part of the earth"*. What *"fourth part"* means could be geographic or quantitative. Which ever, there is a great loss of life by the four active agents; sword, famine, death, wild beasts. These are the implements of war, and the result of war.

Revelation

A look at the history of World Wars I and II show the devastation and human misery that occurs when many nations come together to fight and try to impose their will on one another. Such misery causes an outcry for peace and an end to war. Even so, since these great wars man has been unable to stop war.

6:9, 10   The Fifth Seal. The scene is now changed to an altar which is in heaven, the altar of sacrifice. Under this altar is revealed the *"souls of them that had been slain for the Word of God, and for the testimony which they held"*. It is held by many scholars that these are the Tribulation martyrs, those who were slain during the Great Tribulation (Luke 18:7).

This being the most plain explanation, and if correct, it is therefore evident that the rapture of the faithful Church did not occur at the beginning of the Great Tribulation. Otherwise, where did these souls come from, and how were they saved?

There is much Scriptural support for this position. Read commentary on Daniel 7:1-28 (especially 7:18) and Revelation 7:14. There are other differing views that are far from convincing based on a thorough reference to the whole of the Biblical prophetic Scriptures regarding the Second Coming. A few select verses do not make a case for any position.

As these souls cried out for vengeance they were told, *"to rest yet for a little time"*. There are more *"brethren who should be killed, even as they were"*. The killing of Believers is still in progress at this time. Indicated to those who were crying out is a nearness of the fulfillment and completion of the Apocalypse.

6:12-17   The Sixth Seal. See Matthew 24:29-31 and Joel 2:31. Henry Alford thinks of the saints as going through the Great Tribulation period, and being caught up at the close, just before the Lord descends to earth. Some in the Futurist school thinks of the saints as being caught up before the Great Tribulation period, and the coming of the Lord at the close. The pre-wrath school allows for the saints to be raptured before the *"wrath of God"* - verse 17.
(1 Thess 5:9; Dan 8:19; 11:36)

The events described in these verses reveal the cosmic and earthly convulsions as also described elsewhere in Scripture, that accompany the

end of the present age and the Second Coming of Christ. It seems this calamity on humanity and all creation should occur over a short period of time, perhaps even in one hour, or one day, as Jesus descends and sets His feet on the Mount of Olives.
(Zech 14:4-6; Rev 22:7, 12)

7:1-8   The sealing of the 144,000 from the twelve tribes of Israel and Judah, *"sealed out of every tribe of the children of Israel"* - verse 4. In this vision is seen the activities of angels preparing the chosen ones to represent God as His servants. Some commentators believe the number to be a symbol of full completion (Alford), while others take it literally.

It seems these are *"sealed"*, to be kept from harm during the trials of the Great Tribulation. There is much difference of opinion as exactly to "who" these verses apply; Jews only, or Christians only, or some combination of the two.

The plain teaching is that they are Jewish Believers selected out of every tribe of the children of Israel. When this sealing takes place is not clear. (Joel 2:28-32; 3:1, 2)

7:9-17   John sees, *"a great multitude...standing before the throne... arrayed in white robes..."*. This scene corresponds closely with that described in chapter 4. There is great praise and worship in progress, and John is told by *"one of the elders"* present there, who this great multitude in white robes are; *"these are they that come out of the Great Tribulation, and they washed their robes, and made them white in the blood of the Lamb."* (Matt 24:21, 22) It was through their faith in Christ that their robes were washed and made white.

Scofield offers this astute observation; "The Great Tribulation is a period of unexampled trouble predicted in the passages cited under that head from Psalm 2:5 to Revelation 7:14 and described in Revelation Chapters 11 - 18. Involving in a measure the whole earth (Rev 3:10), it is yet distinctively *"the time of Jacob's trouble"*, (Jer 33:7) and its vortex is Jerusalem and the Holy Land. It involves the people of God (Jews), who will have returned to Palestine in unbelief. Its duration is three and one-half years, or the last half of the Seventieth Week of Daniel."

Dr. Scofield was correct, the "unbelieving" Jews have indeed resettled in Palestine, and the present world conditions point to the soon event of *"the*

Revelation

time of Jacob's trouble", and all the prophetic fulfillments and completions required to allow the Second Coming of Jesus Christ.

The question here is; when and how did this great multitude come to be in heaven *"out of the Great Tribulation?"*. Implied is that they have just come, just before the coming of Christ in judgment, and which, it seems, the Seventh Seal is to be introduced (Chapter 8). There is no reference here to martyrdom, so they may be those who were raptured *"out of the Great Tribulation"*. If so, then the rapture of the faithful Church occurs at some point during the Great Tribulation period, after the midpoint, or near the end, before the wrath of God is poured out.

Campbell Morgan remarks, "I am convinced that not all Christian people will be taken to be with Christ on His return, but only those who by the attitude of their lives are ready for His appearing."

Scofield says, "The Great Tribulation will be, however, a period of salvation...". These comments are disputed; but if they be correct, then the Holy Spirit must be present and active in this "period of salvation" as well. See comments on 2 Thessalonians 2:7.

8:1-6   The Seventh Seal. "Seven", the number of completeness and perfection; the seal is here opened and *"followed a silence in heaven... about half an hour"*. Silence. Not a sound. This *"half an hour"* of silence would seem an eternity, and is a solemn occasion.

This final seal opening reveals the silence, the incense offering, the casting of coals upon the earth, the sounding of the Seven Trumpets and the emptying of the Seven Bowls of Wrath.

"Silence in heaven" - Indicative of the solemn and astonishing things about to happen. It is an anticipation of the fearful unfolding of God's judgments and wrath. *"The Seven Angels"* are receivers of the Seven Trumpets. *"Another angel"* is one who offers incense to mix with the prayers of the saints (Rev 6:9). The answer to these prayers is seen as the bringing of severe judgments upon the earth and the ungodly who persecuted the saints, and kill them (Rev 6:10).

"Cast it upon the earth" - The fire of God's wrath and vengeance upon the ungodly of the earth. The *"thunders, and voices, and lightenings*

and an earthquake" all are symbolic precursors of the coming divine judgments.

8:7   The First Trumpet Judgment. According to Gaebelein, "The Trumpet Judgments would seem to introduce the Great Tribulation proper during the years immediately preceding the coming of Christ to destroy the Antichrist." The first four Trumpets affect the natural objects chiefly, while the other three, the Woe Trumpets, are expressly said to be inflicted upon men (8:13). There is a similarity to the plagues of Egypt recorded in the book of Exodus.

Exactly what is meant by the *"hail and fire, mingled with blood...cast upon the earth"*, is not known. Perhaps the destruction caused results in much man and animal bloodshed becoming mingled in with the hail and fire. The damage caused is wide spread, covering *"the third part of the earth"*. If this be a literal event then such a wide spread natural catastrophe will bring much terror, famine and plague upon the earth. There is given no length of time element here. Could this be a progressive judgment carried out over a considerable period of time, or a one-time event?

8:8, 9   The Second Trumpet Judgment. The plain signification of the text here describes a great pestilence, as *"a great mountain burning with fire was cast into the sea"*. This could very well be a description of a large meteor falling into the sea, causing great destruction. A part of the "celestial disturbances" prophesied for the end times.
(Rev 7:3, 13; Ex 7:20, 21)

8:10, 11   The Third Trumpet Judgment. *"There fell from heaven a great star (called Wormwood)."* The description could very well be a comet, spreading its debris over a third part of the earth. The result is a polluting of water that causes death.
(Rev 7:13; Ex 15:23-25)

8:12, 13   The Fourth Trumpet Judgment. By some unexplained means these celestial disturbances cause the light from the sun, moon and stars to diminish by one-third. This is predicted in Amos 8:9 and Joel 2:2, 10. Perhaps there is a cloud or ash cover over the earth, caused by the previous judgments. Before the next judgments, an eagle flying is heard to cry out, *"woe, woe, woe to the inhabitants of the earth..."*. This is the first time the word *"woe"* is in the Apocalypse.

Revelation

9:1-12   The Fifth Trumpet Judgment and the First Woe. *"A star from heaven"* - most likely Satan himself (Isa 14:12; Luke 10:18). *"The pit of the abyss"* - The present abode of the devil. Alford and others say, "The abyss is not hell, but the present abode of the devil and his angels, including Hades, where the souls of the ungodly dead are awaiting the last judgment. So dense is the smoke rising from the pit that it darkens the sun and the air (6:12; 8:12)."

Satan was given the *"key of the pit"*, and he opened it. *"And out of the smoke came forth locusts."* Wycliffe says, "Locusts are used in the famous prophecy in the book of Joel as symbols of invading armies. Men are likened to locusts in Judges 6:5; Jeremiah 46:23, etc., and in prophetic Scriptures they are symbols of divine judgment (Deut 28:38, 42; Nahum 3:15, 17; Amos 7:1-3; etc.).

They cause great pain and suffering on those who do not have the *"seal of God on their foreheads* (verse 4).*"*

In verses 7-10 is a description of these locusts and in recent times their appearance and sound has been compared to modern day military helicopters. Another view refers these locusts to the ravages of Mohammedanism. The locust itself is peculiarly Arabic, and figurative of the Arabs.

"In the last times many things until then unheard of shall come to pass - much hitherto unseen shall greet mortal eyes" - Hebart. Dusterdieck says, "He, who like Hebart, looks for the literal fulfillment of all these visions, expecting for instance the actual appearance of the locusts described certainly does more justice to the text than does the allegorist." Whatever the view, these are symbols of demon lead powers unleashed on humanity at the time of the end.

9:13-21   The Sixth Trumpet Judgment. The command from the altar to the angel is to *"loose the four angels that are bound...".* These are most likely to be evil angels that have been bound to a specific position, *"prepared for the hour, day and month and year"*. They have an appointed time, specific to *"the hour"*, and an appointed task to perform. Their role is to lead a huge army that, *"kills a third of mankind"*.

Their position of being *"bound at the great river Euphrates"* is significant. In Daniel 10:12-14 is found spiritual warfare between *"the prince of the Persian kingdom"*, and *"Michael, one of the chief princes (archangel)"*, that lasted for *"twenty-one days"*. In verse 20 the angel Michael tells Daniel that, *"Soon I will return to fight against the prince of Persia..."*. This is the land of the Babylonians and the great Euphrates River, the land of modern Iraq and Iran. All chastisements of Israel have come from this region.

This spiritual warfare at this location seems to be a continuing confrontation between the angels of God and the evil angels of Satan. Among the ancient commentators it was almost their universal opinion that Antichrist was to arise from this region. It is from this area that Mohammed began the religion of Islam.

In verse 16 is given the *"number of the armies"*. It is a staggering number: 200,000,000! Whether this is a literal number, or a schematic representation of this huge army, it is a very large military force. Most likely it contains men from many nations and nationalities, and their goal is the destruction and plundering of Israel. Reference Ezekiel 38:1-23. Moorehead says, "This great army is human, and not a countless multitude of evil spirits, as some think. It may be the imperial army of the Antichrist and possibly consist of mainly Mohammedans."

Petingill says, "It refers to the nations of the world gathered against Israel to cut them off from national existence." It is not a stretch at all to see these Bible scholars of old being very astute in their studied understanding of prophetic Scriptures and the workings of future literal events.

The descriptions of the great army raise many questions. Nobody knows for sure, but this comment from Elliott is interesting. He says, "These descriptions suit well the uniforms of the Turkish army". Turkey is due north of Israel. Present day events have Turkey and Israel relations very strained, and Turkey is a Moslem country, aligned strongly with Russia. See commentary on Ezekiel 38:1-23.

Even with the killing of *"one-third of mankind"*, with strong and devastating plagues, still there was no repentance, for mankind *"repented not"*. Ludhardt says, "Such moral corruption will occur at the end in spite of advanced culture; for culture itself does not promote morality, but as history teaches, may be employed as well in the service of ungodliness and immorality."

This is certainly a true statement, as is easily observed in the historical affairs of mankind. Listening to a classical music symphony, dressed in polite

Revelation

finery, all the while murdering the innocent Jewish families, as occurred in Hitler's Nazi Germany during World War II. Or, in more recent times, America's decades of murder of the unborn via legalized, government approved abortion. Verse 21, *"They repented not of their murders..."*. Such is the state of ungodliness today.

10:1-11   The Strong Angel and the Little Book. Here begins a parenthetical passage between the Sixth and Seventh Trumpets. (Chapters 10:1 to 11:14) Verse 1 describes in some detail *"another strong angel"* who is a messenger of divine judgment. *"He had in his hand a little book open..."* - a little scroll. The image of the angels presence is over the earth and sea - the whole of the earth, but perhaps especially over Palestine and the Mediterranean Sea. John heard voices speaking, but was told to not record what was uttered. There has been much speculation what was revealed, but no one knows for sure what *"the seven thunders uttered"*.

Verse 6 declares by *"Him who lives forever...who created the heavens...the earth, etc., there shall be no more delay!"* This pronouncement stated the fact that the next Trumpet was to issue in the reign of Christ and His saints. Verse 7 plainly says that the fulfillment of all prophecy is to occur at the time of the Seventh Trumpet. The appointed time of delay is at an end! Weidner says, "This finishing of the mystery of God is the glorious consummation of God's Kingdom when the kingdoms of the world shall have become the kingdoms of our Lord and His Christ, when He shall reign forever and ever." (Rev 11:15-18)

John was told to take the little scroll and eat it. It was *"bitter and sweet"*; sour in the stomach, but sweet in the mouth. He was told to *"prophesy again about the many peoples and nations and tongues and kings"*. Perhaps the little book contained the remaining chapters of the Revelation. For the Believer it is to be eternally sweet; for the ungodly it is eternally bitter.

11:1, 2   The Temple Restored. John was told to measure *"the temple of God and the altar, and count the worshipers there"*. Some early Bible commentators advocated the teaching that Jerusalem will be inhabited again, the temple rebuilt, then the city sacked by the Gentiles. They were, and are, no doubt correct.

Fausset said, "The literal temple shall be rebuilt on the return of the Jews to their land." These commentators, who in times past believed the prophetic Scriptures and understood the literalness of prophecy, should be in the forefront today as great Scriptural scholars.

"The Gentiles will trample the city for forty - two months." This, and the 1260 days, and the three and one-half years doubtless are periods of the same length, but not necessarily the same period of time. The time here mentioned is literally the last half of the Seventieth Week of Daniel's vision, the days of Antichrist after he profaned the temple in Jerusalem, and set himself up as god.
(Dan 7:25; 8:11, 12-19; 9:24-27; 11:29-32, 36; 12:11; 2 Thess 2:3, 4)

11:3-12   The Two Witnesses. Literally, two individual men, probably well known to John. The fact that they are clothed in sackcloth strongly favors the literal interpretation.

No doubt these men preach repentance and the approaching judgment. They are to be empowered and preserved by God for the specified time of 1260 days.

"When they shall have finished their testimony the Beast...shall kill them." The time of their prophesy is most likely during the first half of the times of the Antichrist. This is the first mention of the "Beast", and evidently is the same as mentioned in 13:1 and 17:8 (Dan 7:8-21). Weidner says, "This Beast is evidently the Antichrist who now manifests himself in all his diabolical power as the Man of Sin." (2 Thess 2:3, 4)

After the two witnesses are killed by the Antichrist, their bodies lay in place for three and one-half days in Jerusalem. The inhabitants of the earth rejoice and celebrate by sending each other gifts (verse 10). There is no repentance shown, as the wicked people considered these men as their tormentors. God resuscitates the two *"dead witnesses"*, and they go up to heaven in a cloud, as a terrified world looks on, and hears a loud voice from heaven say, *"Come up here"*.

In earlier commentaries this ability of the whole world to *"look upon - gaze on their bodies"* (verse 9) was a real puzzle, and impossible to understand. Now it is easily possible to understand, with the worldwide availability of satellite television news and the internet; this "impossible to understand" prophecy of earlier times is, indeed, today literally possible. The prophetic

Revelation

Scriptures literalness continues to show the Sovereignty and Omnipresence of God in His Word, and the affairs of this world.

11:13, 14   The Second Woe. A severe earthquake comes immediately after the translation of the two witnesses to heaven, and *"seven thousand persons are killed"* in Jerusalem. *"The survivors were terrified and gave glory to God in heaven."* Of this comment Wycliffe says, "We detect no conviction of sin here, merely a sense of fear, which soon passes." Verse 14 - *"The Second Woe has passed; the third one is coming soon."*

11:15-19   The Seventh Trumpet Judgment. *"And the seventh angel sounded."* Alford calls attention to the fact that, "The seventh member in each series of visions, seals, trumpets and bowls, are all differently accompanied from any of the preceding series in each case:

   (a.) At each seventh member we hear what is done not on the earth, but in heaven.
   (b.) Each seventh member is followed by the statement that there followed voices, thunders, lightenings, and earthquake.
   (c.) At each seventh member it is plainly indicated that the end is come, or close at hand."

"All this", Alford says, "forms grounds for inference that the three series of visions are not continuous but resumptive (to resume after an interruption); not indeed, going over the same ground with one another, either of time or occurrence, but each evolving something that was not in the former, and putting the course of God's Providence in a different light. They are not, then to be thought of as merely occurring in temporal succession."

The verses here plainly reveal the finality of the judgments and of heavens sovereignty over the earth. (12:10; 17:14) Fausset says this, as do others, "That here begins the Millennial reign, the consummation of the majesty of God." This trumpet sound proclaims the end of the Great Tribulation as well, and says Seiss, "The Seventh Trumpet is the last trumpet, at the sound of which the dead are raised and the prophets and saints receive their rewards (20:11-15)." Then the voice declares, *"The Kingdom of this world is become the Kingdom of our Lord and His Christ."*
(Dan 7:14; 1 Cor 15:24-28)

In verse 19 is seen *"God's temple in heaven was opened, and within His temple was seen the ark of the covenant."* Wycliffe says, "This verse should be considered as the introduction to what is about to be revealed in Chapter 12. What John sees presents a problem in interpretation. What is this 'ark' he describes, and the sanctuary in which it resides? When the Holy City descends from heaven, it is explicitly said that there is no temple seen there (21:22)."

There is no need to speculate, as the answer lies in the future fulfillment and revelation at another time.

12:1-17   The Woman and the Dragon. After the Seventh Trumpet has sounded, John goes back and starts again with a fresh vision. This vision may be more symbolic and descriptive rather than prophetical, and relating to things past and passing.

The content appears to be a heavenly view of the birth of Christ. Here is seen another battle between Michael and his angels against the devil and his angels. The result of this war was Satan and his angels lost their place in heaven. Their abode and place of evil activity became the earth. *"He (Satan) is filled with fury, because he knows that his time is short."*

There are various interpretations, and so many different opinions about this that it seems best to make no detailed comments, except to say that what is seen in verses 10-12 is a song of rejoicing. Emphasis is upon the power of God and the authority of Christ. The Believers overcame Satan, *"the accuser"*, because of the sacrifice *"by the blood of the Lamb, and the word of the Believers testimony."*

In verse 17 is revealed Satan's rage against *"the rest of her offspring"*, no doubt meaning those who are the children of God; Believers, who obey God and whose testimony stays strong in the face of persecution and death. If *"offspring"* also relates to the Jewish people, then according to Gaebelein, he refers them to the godly remnant in the land of Palestine, perhaps to the 144,000 sealed ones during the Great Tribulation.

13:1-10   The Beast out of The Sea. The description of this Beast (the dragon, the Antichrist), which is the same as that in Chapter 17, and the fourth beast in Daniel Chapter 7. He is given great authority to rule *"for forty-two months"*, (verse 5) to blaspheme God and all that dwell in heaven (verse 6). See comments on Daniel 7:8.

Revelation

13:7   *"And it was given to him authority to make war with the saints, and to overcome them...authority over every tribe... people...tongue... nation."* See comments on Daniel Chapter 7.

Weidner remarks, "Though many shall fall away and worship the Beast, even among professing Christians, the True Believers shall be preserved through (or exempted from - according to the exegesis adopted) the Great Tribulation."

At this present time there seems to be many "professing Christians" whose support of ungodly worldly views; such as abortion, homosexuality, immoral lifestyles, dependence on human governments and their leaders, enjoying the profanity and immorality of "Hollywood", worship of material things, etc., show a lack of understanding and/or acceptance of the Biblical and Godly view of life. This is strong evidence of the final great apostasy and "falling away" mentioned in Scripture that is to occur at the very end of days. See comments, Matt 24:9-12.

The born again (John 3:3) Believer is to *"present yourself to God as one approved, a workman who does not need to be ashamed, and who correctly handles the word of truth"* - 2 Timothy 2:13. In Ephesians 4:1 Paul *"urges"* the Believer *"to live a life worthy of the calling you have received"*. Ephesians Chapter 4 through Chapter 6, gives Paul's instructions to *"the faithful in Christ Jesus"* to better understand what is expected as the behavior of the Believer.

Ephesians 5:6, 7 gives this admonition: *"Let no one deceive you...God's wrath comes on those who are disobedient...do not be partners* (partakers in their sins) *with them."* As true followers of Jesus, the Believer is expected, and in many ways, commanded, to live a life pleasing to God. To do otherwise puts one at a high risk of "being deceived" and coming under the wrath of God in these last days. Ignorance is no excuse - Romans 1:18-20.

For assurance of our *"knowing Him"*, who is *"the atoning sacrifice for our sins"*, the Apostle John says in 1 John 2:3, *"We know that we have come to know Him if we obey His commands"*. "Christianity requires moral conduct, not just intellectual attainment." - Wycliffe.

1 John 2:6 proclaims: *"Whoever claims to live in Him must* (ought) *walk as Jesus did."* (Matt 11:28, 29; John13:15; Phil 2:5-8; 1 Pet 2:21) This is done in the Believer by the power of the indwelling Holy Spirit and knowing what behaviors are displeasing to Him, and by the dedication each Believer makes to *"confess our sins,* (as) *He is faithful and just and will forgive our sins and purify us from all unrighteousness"* - 1 John 1:8. (Rom 3:21-31)

13:8   *"All the inhabitants of the earth will worship the beast..."* This points to the great final rebellion and apostasy as predicted by Jesus in Matthew 24:10. The exception to this worship is that all who belong to *"the Lamb that was slain"* will not worship the Beast, or his image, or take his mark. Their names are *"written in the book of life."* (Rev 20:4, 12)

13:10   The Greek text here is uncertain. This verse is a warning to Believers to suffer with patience and expectation that God will avenge the elect. *"Patient endurance and faithfulness"* is called for by the saints.

13:11-18   The Beast out of The Earth. This second beast, an accomplice of the first, leading people to worship him, seems to be a personification of false prophecy.
(Rev 16:13; 19:20; 20:10; Matt 24:11, 24)

In verse 12 this beast causes the inhabitants of earth to *"worship the first beast, whose death stroke is healed."* This event is an enigma, but its result is great awe and adoration of the Antichrist as *"the whole earth wondered after the beast"* (13:4) and *"who is able to war with him?"* He must be considered invincible by most of those living in his time.

The second beast was given power to perform miracles and signs (13:13, 14) so that by these diabolical miracles the worldly minded are deceived. In some manner not yet understood he was to *"make an image of the beast...that it should speak...and cause those who do not worship the beast to be killed."* There are speculations about how this is done, but this again is an enigma.

Verses 16 - 18 reveal another enigma. The Antichrist rule will include economic power* to control all commerce, so that *"no man should be able to buy or sell, save he has the mark"*, known as the "mark of the Beast". This mark is to be visible, on the hand or forehead, and in some manner contains *"the number of his name (666)."*

---

* The Strategy, Policy and Review Department of the International Monetary Fund recommends that the world adopt a global currency called the "Bancor" and that a global central bank be established to administer that currency. The report is dated April 13, 2010.

There are many speculations regarding this number, and to whom it applies. Only in due time will Believers be able to recognize him by this number. Believers should beware of efforts to be identified by some physical "mark" until the Antichrist is fully revealed and this mystery of the *"mark"* solved. (2 Thess 2:3, 4)

14:1-5   <u>The Lamb and the 144,000.</u> This chapter contains seven visions recording apparently the main events of the closing days of this age. Terrible judgments are about to occur and the visions are given to prepare people for them. Salvation may still be possible - 14:6, 7.

"The purpose of this first vision of the 144,000 redeemed standing with the Lamb on Mount Zion, (in heaven?), is to give Believers who are on earth courage and patience, that if they, too, remain faithful through all the persecutions by Antichrist (Rev 13:7), then they also shall attain to the glory described in these verses" - Dusterdieck.

There is some dispute regarding the location of Mount Zion; in heaven or the earthly location. This is especially a difficult vision to interpret. It is thought by most expositors that the scene is in heaven, and the 144,000 are especially set apart as being unusually dedicated, stamped for identity and with understanding of heavenly song and music, not defiled with women, and they follow the Lamb everywhere He goes. They are the first fruits of God without blemish. This is no doubt a select group of God's saints of which we hear nothing more.

Perhaps these are they who, as the first fruits, *"redeemed from the earth"* as special Jewish saints come out of the Tribulation time. (Rev 7:4-9; Rom 8:23; 1 Cor 15:23)

14:6, 7   The Angel With the Everlasting Gospel. This angel comes *"to proclaim unto them that dwell on the earth...the hour of His judgment is come"*. The glory and eternal Gospel is announced to all people on the earth at this time, the latter days. Special emphasis is given to the fact that worship is to be given to God, *"who made the heavens and the earth"*, which is denied by most today, as the theory of evolution permeates education and ridicules the idea of creation by God. Implicit is a challenge to the worship being given to the Antichrist.

14:8   Babylon the Great Judged. Most likely this refers to the chief city of Antichrist, and/or the seat of world power which persecutes the Church. See Chapters 17 - 18. (Jer 51:7-9)

14:9-12   Judgment on the Beast Worshippers.

This is the most dreadful of all threatenings in Scripture;

"If any one worships the Beast and his image and receives the mark on the forehead or hand, he, too, will drink of the wine of God's fury, which has been poured full strength into the cup of His wrath. He will be tormented with burning sulphur in the presence of the holy angels and the Lamb. And the smoke of their torment rises forever and ever. There is no rest day or night for those who worship the Beast and his image, or for anyone who receives the mark of his name." (Rev 20:4)

A careful consideration of exactly what is revealed here is truly sobering. There is no element of grace, mercy, hope or compassion blended with this judgment. The punishment is extreme, eternal and deserved.

The recipients of this judgment have had ample warning and opportunity to repent and not follow the Antichrist, but refused.
(Rev 6:13-17; 9:20, 21; 13:8)

As in Genesis 3:1, the great deceiver will challenge this and other revelations from God...*"Did God really say?"*. It is of eternal consequence that all Believers be educated and understand that, yes, God's word really does pronounce severe and eternal punishment on those who accept the lies and deceit of the Antichrist, so as to follow and worship him, his image, and take his "mark". As Jesus frequently said, *"He who has ears let him hear..."*

Revelation

Verse 12 calls for *"patient endurance of the part of the saints who obey God's commandments and remain faithful to Jesus"*. The theme in Scripture seems very consistent; Believer, do not be lead away from the true Gospel, as you will be severely tested and persecuted in the end times. By most all Scripture indications the *"saints"* will endure part, or all of the Great Tribulation, and the persecutions that come during the reign of the Antichrist, except the *"wrath of God"*.

In verse 13, *"a voice from heaven"* pronounced, *"Blessed are the dead who die in the Lord from now on"*. This seems a peculiar blessing on those who maintain faith and are honored for their *"labors"* after the revealing of Antichrist and his mark. It leads up to the "harvest" in the following verses.

14:14-20   The Harvest of the Earth. The time for a triumphant Christ is come, to begin judgment as the *"earth is ripe"* and *"the earth was reaped"*. There are indicated here two reapings.

In verse 16 the harvest seems to be the gathering of the elect. Moorehead says, "1 Thessalonians 4:13-18 is another account of this majestic scene, the gathering of God's people into His everlasting Kingdom by resurrection and translation. This does not occur before the Great Tribulation, but it does occur before the wrath of God is poured out."
(Isa 26:20; Rom 5:8, 9; 1 Thess 5:9)

The fact that there seems to be two reapings, and that the former seems to be over before the latter begins, favors the thought that there are two classes of those reaped. (Matt 13:24-30, 37-43)

Verses 17-20 describe the harvest of the ungodly and their destruction in *"the great winepress of God's wrath"*. (Jer 25:30-38; Rev 19:15) This is the terrific nature of the punishment that shall overtake the enemies of Christ at the time of His coming to destroy the Antichrist (Rev 19:11-21). "The battle of Armageddon comes now into view for the first time" - Gaebelein. (Joel 3:1-3, 12-16)

It appears that the harvest of the Believers at the rapture will occur just before the events of verses 17-20. In verses 14-16 the first harvester is Christ, and the second harvest in verse 19 is by angels only. This seems to confirm that the first harvest is of the Believers, and the second immediately following is of the ungodly for judgment. Verse 18 shows one angel comes *"from the altar".* This is the same altar of incense beneath which the souls of the martyrs lie crying out for vengeance. (Rev 6:9; 8:3; 16:7)

15:1-8   The Seven Angels With Seven Plagues. In verse 1 is seen the overview; seven angels with the seven last plagues that complete God's wrath. Verses 2-4 contain a scene in heaven of those who are *"victorious over the Beast",* and in gratitude and praise *"they sing the song of Moses...and the song of the Lamb".* These two songs perhaps represent the joy of redeemed Jews as well as Gentiles. The chapter concludes with the description of the *"seven angels with the seven plagues".* They were given *"seven golden bowls filled with the wrath of God",* to complete the destruction of the ungodly wicked.

Fausset says, "The elect, after their trials, especially those arising from the Beast, shall be taken up before the vials (bowls) of wrath are poured on the Beast and his kingdom. The Lord coming with the clouds in flaming fire, shall first catch up His elect people and then shall destroy the enemy."

16:1-21   The Seven Bowls of God's Wrath. The pouring out of these bowls may all occur during the blowing of the Seventh Trumpet. Wycliffe comments that the blowing of the Seventh Trumpet was delayed until the Seventh Bowl was to be poured. Alford says, "There can then be no doubt here, not only that the series reaches on to the time of the end, but that the whole of it is to be placed very close to the end time. It belongs by its very condition to the time of the end."

Weidner remarks, "God now begins a direct way to bring to an end the Great Tribulation through which His faithful ones are passing, by visiting judgment upon the followers of Antichrist." Other commentators refer these signs and events to the time preceding the Second Coming as the woes and convulsions of nature spoken of by the Lord in Matthew 24:29 and Luke 21:11.

There is much speculation about these bowl events. They seem to be patterned somewhat after the plagues on Egypt before the Exodus. The descriptions suggest that the fulfillments may be literal, but the future alone must decide the question.

The First Bowl - Painful sores on those with the mark of the Beast, and who worship his image.

Revelation

The Second Bowl - Sea turned to blood, and every living thing in the sea died.

The Third Bowl - Rivers and springs turned to blood.

The Fourth Bowl - Intense heat from the sun.

The Fifth Bowl - Darkness on the Beast's kingdom and his followers refuse to repent.

The Sixth Bowl - Euphrates River dried up to prepare a way for the Kings of the East to assemble at Armageddon for their own destruction. The vast hordes of Asia will attend the great day of God.

The Seventh Bowl - *"It is done!".* Great upheavals occur with a changing of the whole earth, giant hailstones pound the people still remaining, who continue to curse God. The Antichrist and his followers are destroyed. (Ezk 38:22)

This brief summary of the Bowl Judgments do not, of course, reflect the many ideas about these events, and all the details that can be interpreted in a variety of ways. Some commentators believe the events are only symbolic and not literal. An example is that the size of the hailstones in verse 21 is interpreted to be 57 - 96 pounds! Previously a size unknown, huge and destructive by any measure. In any event the end times will separate God's faithful from the ungodly who, *"curse God on account of the plague of hail..."*. This cursing of God seems to indicate a literal hail event of great magnitude and destruction.

17:1-6   The Woman on the Beast. Here is another enigma wrapped in a mystery. The *"punishment of the great prostitute"* is to be shown in Chapter 18. In these verses she is introduced as one *"who sits on many waters"*. Verse 15 shows that by *"waters"* is meant *"peoples, and multitudes, and nations and tongues"*, over which she ruled.

Who is this great harlot? There are many speculations and ideas about who, where, what do all the symbols and things stated mean.

Wycliffe comments that historically she is identified with the papacy. No doubt she represents some vast spiritual system that persecutes the true saints of God. She enters into relations with governments of the earth, and for a while rules them.

She is spiritually false and exercises an evil influence in the name of religion. Both the woman and the beast are each one a complex mystery that caused the Apostle John to *"wonder"*.

Her role in the end time events, as a part of the anti-Christian confederacy, is stated very clearly in verse 6 - *"I saw that the woman was drunk with the blood of the saints, the blood of those who bore the testimony of Jesus."*

The great harlot therefore must operate as a merciless and ruthless "killing machine" for the Antichrist.

What religion in the world today openly hates Christians and Jews, the people of God? Islam. Not just radical Islam, but the stated religion of Islam as defined by their leader, Mohammed, and what he wrote in the Koran.

The "moderate" Muslims who live among Christians today have, for the most part, not spoken out against their "radical" brothers. Their silence reflects their fear of reprisal from within their own religion, as well as a comfort with the persecutions of any religion but their own. All beliefs other than Islam are considered as "infidel". Infidels must be converted to Islam or killed.

Muslims are rapidly infiltrating the Western Nations of the world, and increasing their numbers and influence worldwide. Refer to the following report about Muslim population growth.

The world's Muslim population is expected to increase by about 35% in the next 20 years, rising from 1.6 billion in 2010 to 2.2 billion by 2030, according to new population projections by the Pew Research Center's Forum on Religion & Public Life.

Globally, the Muslim population is forecast to grow at about twice the rate of the non- Muslim population over the next two decades – an average annual growth rate of 1.5% for Muslims, compared with 0.7% for non-Muslims. If current trends continue, Muslims will make up 26.4% of the world's total projected population of 8.3 billion in 2030, up from 23.4% of the estimated 2010 world population of 6.9 billion.

- The Pew Forum on Religion and Public Life: The Future of the Global Muslim Population, January 27, 2011

Revelation

17:7-18   In these verses the angel tells John, *"I will explain to you the mystery of the woman and of the beast she rides, which has seven heads and ten horns".* Now comes the challenge to understand the riddle; *"Here is the mind that has wisdom"* - verse 9. The angel begins to present a problem which is utterly impossible to solve to general satisfaction.

There are very many interpretations and arguments regarding what is meant by the information revealed in verses 8-18. The one most common denominator in all the various proposals of interpretation is about the apostate church of the end times. (Rev 18:4) Suffice it to say as time unrolls the scroll of history, the meaning of these prophecies will become known.

18:1-8   <u>God's People Warned to Come Out.</u> *"Another angel... having great authority..."* makes this announcement *"with a mighty voice"*, that Babylon is fallen and is now inhabited by *"demons and unclean spirits".* She is to be entirely desolate, as described of the old city of Babylon in Isaiah 13:10-22. In verse 3 the angel describes the extent of her power and worldly influence.

Fausset comments, "That the reference is not to earthly merchandise, but to spiritual wares, to indulgences, idolatries, superstitions, worldly compromises, etc., wherewith the harlot, the apostate church, has made merchandise out of people."

18:4   *"Another voice from heaven"* - an angel speaking, in the name of Christ, to the saints of God to *"come out of her"*, to not mingle, not have fellowship so as to be found guilty of her sins and incur God's wrath that is fast approaching (verse 5). The destruction of this apostate religion, the harlot, the *"mother of prostitutes and of the abominations of the earth"* (Rev 17:5) who was *"drunk with the blood of the saints, those who bore the testimony of Jesus"*, will be accomplished in *"one day"* (verse 8). Such a rapid and complete destruction is easily accomplished in this present time with nuclear weapons.

There will be a severe calamity befall the harlot who sits *"as queen"* (verse 7), as the Antichrist and his allies execute God's wrath on her and her city (Rev 17:16, 17; 18:20-24) When the *"kings of the earth who committed adultery with her, and the merchants of the earth (who) grew rich from her excessive luxuries"*, see *"the smoke of her burning...they weep and mourn over her."*

18:9-19   The Fall of Babylon. These verses describe the wealth of the city, the merchandise bought and sold, and the grief of the worlds merchants who have been made rich by this city and system. In verse 17, *"Every sea captain... sailors...will stand far off, when they see the smoke of her burning"*. This must refer to a seacoast city of great size and enterprise that provides the worlds merchants with products and wealth.

What and where is this city? There have been several candidates submitted over time; a restored Babylon, London, Paris, Rome, and more recently New York City. If taken literally as a geographic location, then London, New York City, or Rome seem best to fit.

New York City has been targeted already by the possible people of the Antichrist, the Moslems, who hate God's people, both Jews and Christians. Almost 1,500,000 Jews live there presently. New York City is also home of the United Nations, which is actively working to establish a one-world community and global religious system.

See comments on Revelation 17:1-6. See Addendum for information about the United Nations.

Some commentators make "Babylon", stand for the papacy as the world religion that has betrayed Christianity, and is interlocked with the pagan, godless governments of the world in the end times. This compromising relationship will lead the Antichrist, who believes himself to be god, to need to destroy all religion except those who worship him and his image.

There is, today, among Moslems, the expected arrival of the "Twelfth Imam", who is their version of the end time Moslem Messiah who comes in power and authority to subdue the "infidels", and rule the world.

Muhammad al-Mahdī also known as *Hujjat ibn al-Hasan* (approximately July 29, 869 – ?) believed by twelvers to be the individual believed by Twelver Shī'a Muslims to be the Māhdī, an ultimate savior of humankind and the final Imam of the Twelve Imams.

Revelation

Twelver Shī'a believe that al-Māhdī was born in 869 and did not die but rather was hidden by God (this is referred to as the Occultation) and will later emerge with Jesus in order to fulfill their mission of bringing peace and justice to the world. He assumed the Imamate at 5 years of age. Sunnīs and other Shī'ah schools do not consider ibn-al-Hasan to be the Māhdī, though the mainstream sect Twelvers do.   - wikipedia.org

---

This has been alluded to by the present leadership in Iran, as a part of their end time activities in developing nuclear weapons, to bring destruction on Israel and America to facilitate the coming of this Mahdi, the Twelfth Imam.

18:20-24   Heaven Rejoices Over the Destruction of Babylon. Those who dwell in heaven rejoice over God's judgment on her, Babylon. The "great city...shall be found no more". The destruction is total annihilation, sudden and complete. No more music, no more life of pleasure, business or personal.

Weidner says, "The future Babylon, the great world city of the last days, will be the central power from which all the persecutions of the saints will arise, especially in the earlier part of the Antichrists reign, before Babylon is destroyed by him and his allied kings."

Perhaps the Antichrist doesn't need his killing machine (17:1-6), "the harlot, Babylon", anymore because the remaining saints have been raptured out (verse 20) from the earth, before God's wrath commences. (1 Thess 1:10; 5:9) In the following chapter 19:1 is heard "the voice of a great multitude" and "the marriage of the Lamb is come". (19:7)

19:1-6   Hallelujah of the Heavenly Multitude. Almighty God is praised for salvation and justice by this great multitude of the united hosts of heaven; angels, prophets, apostles, saints. In addition the twenty elders and the four living creatures fall down in worship and praise to God.

19:7-10   The Marriage of the Lamb. The privilege of the Church, who "has made herself ready" for the marriage. The attire of the bride, the Church, is "fine linen, bright and pure". Her "righteous acts" is the covering as fine linen. Those who are invited are considered "blessed".

This marriage is introduced here, and the full and final consummation is in Chapter 21, after the overthrow of the Beast, and the binding of Satan, and the general judgment of Chapter 20.

"The elect Church", says Fausset, "is transfigured at the Lord's coming and joins with Him in His triumph over the Beast."

Most commentators maintain that the "Marriage of the Lamb" and the joyous marriage festivities take place at the beginning of the Millennium reign, but others refer it to after the final defeat of Gog and Magog at the end of the Millennium.

In verse 10 is a lesson in whom worship is to be given. Fausset says, "John, intending to worship the angel here, as in 22:8, is the involuntary impulse of adoring joy at so blessed a prospect as that portrayed by the angel. It exemplifies the corrupt tendencies of our fallen nature that even John, an Apostle, gave in and voluntarily worshipped an angel, which Paul warned against doing." (Col 2:18) God alone is worthy of worship. (Matt 4:10; John 4:24; Rev 14:7)

19:11-16   The Rider on the White Horse. The vision of the Second Coming of Christ in glory is revealed here, as John *"saw the heavens opened"*. In 17:3 John in Spirit was carried to the earth, so his vision most likely is from that vantage point. The rider on the white horse is none other than Christ, and shows His departure from heaven to smite the Antichrist by *"a stone cut without hands"* - Daniel 2:34, 35. It is this coming of Christ in glory, with His saints and angels (Zech 6:1-8), that will deliver the Jewish remnant (Rom 11; Isa 11:11; Jer 23:5, 6). "This battle is the first event of the 'Day of Jehovah'." - Scofield

In verses 12 and 13 is given a vivid description of the *"King of kings"*, as He is going forth to conquer His enemies (Isa 63:3-6; 62:11, 12). In verse 13 Jesus is named *"the Word of God"*. Wycliffe comments, "As the Word of God, he made the worlds. It was by rejection of the Word that sin was brought into the world. By the Word of God, salvation is offered to men."

The *"armies of heaven were following Him...dressed in fine linen"*. These are the glorified saints, the true Believers, as described in verses 6-8. Most likely this army of saints accompany Christ as mere joyful spectators of His victory, as He executes the wrath of God on His enemies (verse 15).

Revelation

Jesus Christ is able to conquer His enemies without man's help, as He is *"King of kings and Lord of lords."* (Dan 8:25)

19:17-21   The Battle of Armageddon. The word "Armageddon" is now part of the English language and is defined as "the place of the last decisive battle". How foolish man has become, as the rulers of the whole world are united in one terrible effort to destroy the anointed One of God, who came to offer salvation and reconciliation out of God's great love and mercy toward humanity. (Psalm 2) How very arrogant and psychotic the worlds rulers and their followers are to become, thinking they are masters of the world.
(Isa 2:9-11; Jer 50:31; Dan 8:23-25)

This battle is considered by most all scholars to be a literal event. It is to take place on the famous plain of Megiddo, also called the plain of Jezreel, or Esdraelon. There have been many battles in history fought on these grounds, from Barak and Gideon in the Bible, to British General Allenby's great victory against the Turks in 1917. He was later honored with the title, Lord Allenby of Megiddo.

Prophecies that refer to this coming great battle are found as early as 800 BC. (Joel 3:9-15; Jer 51:27-36; Zeph 3:8; Rev 14:14-20; 16:13-16; 17:14) The battle is over quickly. The Beast and False Prophet are captured and *"thrown alive into the fiery lake of burning sulphur"*. The Gehenna, or Hell, properly so-called (Matt 5:22).

Later Satan and Death and Hades are cast into the same place. This is the second death. (Rev 20:10, 14)

The slaughter is great, as *"the rest of them were killed"*.
(Ezk 39:12-16) The great army of the nations that followed Antichrist is slain, to be feasted upon by the birds of the earth. There must be very many birds present at that time. (Ezk 39:17-20) Wild animals also participate in the feeding.

20:1-3   Satan Bound for a Thousand Years. An angel from heaven secures Satan in *"the abyss"*. Satan is completely *"sealed"* and banished from earth. Sin still exists in individuals, but it is no longer a power in fellowship with Satan for one thousand years. He is no longer able to *"deceive the nations"*.

It is clearly implied here that after the destruction of Antichrist in Revelation 19:21, there will remain nations on earth who did not take part in the conflict. At the end of the one thousand year banishment Satan *"must be loosed for a little time".* (Rev 20:7, 8)

20:4-6   The First Resurrection. Of this resurrection Wycliffe says, "The first resurrection may easily be considered as occurring in stages: the dead in Christ, then we who are alive, and then, after a brief period, these martyrs and faithful ones of the Tribulation period." See also comments on 1 Thessalonians 4:13-18.

John saw *"thrones, and they that sat upon them..."*. There are different views about who are the occupants on the thrones. The preferred view is that they are the twelve Apostles as in Matthew 19:28, and the saints. (1 Cor 6:2, 3) The judgment *"given to them"* is on whom? Christians *"shall judge angels"*. 2 Timothy 2:12 says that saints *"shall sit down with the Redeemer upon His throne"*. Matthew 19:28 says the Apostles *"shall sit on thrones and judge the twelve tribes of Israel"*.

John also sees in this same scene the *"souls of those who had been beheaded..."*. Here are the martyrs from out of the Tribulation who maintained their *"testimony for Jesus"*. It must be noted that Islam beheads "infidels". They seem to enjoy doing it publicly.

Also coming to reign with Christ are those who refused to worship the Beast or his image, and that had not taken his mark. *"They came to life and reigned with Christ a thousand years."* It is not stated where they reigned, in heaven or on earth, but since they *"came to life"* it seems they may be on earth during the thousand years. *"The rest of the dead did not come to life until the thousand years were ended."* One thousand years in Latin is "Millennium." The Roman numeral "M" meaning one thousand. There is no good reason for rejecting the literal meaning here.

"The rest of the dead" is debated whether this means pious dead, wicked dead, or both. Also to be considered are those who die during the Millennium. In any case here is declared, *"This is the first resurrection"*, referring to those *"blessed and holy"* who are to reign with Christ during the one thousand years. *"The second death"* takes place at the final judgment. (Verse 14)

20:7-10   Satan's Doom. The end of evil! "In the providence of God, Satan is once again permitted to turn his demoniacal power against

Revelation

the Church, God's people, that the glory of God may be manifested in Satan's irrecoverable overthrow. The reign of the saints does not cease and it is highly probable that this final struggle will be as brief as it is fierce." - Weidner

The apostate nations living still in the Millennium are deceived and assembled to war by Satan, who leads them against *"the camp of God's people"*. This is the *"Gog and Magog"* army, numerous as *"the sand on the seashore"*. (Ezekiel Chapters 38 and 39) These many peoples are marching into the jaws of sudden and complete death. *"Fire came down from heaven and devoured them."*

Since they are *"devoured"* by fire there are needed no *"birds to feast on them"*, as there was at Antichrist defeat in Revelation 19:21.

Their judgment is sudden, swift, overwhelming, and final, as is the fate of Satan, the devil, as he is *"thrown into the lake of burning sulphur, where the Beast and False Prophet had been thrown. They will be tormented day and night, forever and ever"*.

Wycliffe concludes, "The question is often asked; how can one account for this last rebellion after the beneficent Millennial reign of Christ? For one thing, it reveals that a thousand years of imprisonment does not alter the evil character of Satan, the devil.

Furthermore, unregenerate humanity does not change, and although the whole world is under the rule of Christ, great multitudes obey Him only from fear and not from love, as a follower of Him." This just again proves how foolish the mind of man can be, and how easily deceived. The foolish pride and arrogance of some people cannot be "regenerated"! The reprobate mind is set against God.
(Matt 7:6; John 8:42-47; Rom 2:8-10; 2 Pet 2:12)

20:11-15   The Last Judgment. From Wycliffe: "The judgment of the impenitent dead. A day of judgment, sometimes called "the Last Day", is referred to more often by the Lord than by all the Apostles and their writings put together. (Matt 10:15; 11:22-24; 12:36; John 5:28, 29; 6:39-54; 11:24; Heb 9:27; 10:27)"

"Christ is everywhere identified as the judge. (Acts 17:31; John 5:22-27; 1 Tim 4:1) This event brings the present age of human history to its climax."

Wycliffe continues, "No one will be able to escape this judgment. Death itself, it seems, is not abolished until the Great White Throne is set up, and human destiny is forever settled. Belief in the joy and promises of eternal glory as revealed in the Bible must also bring belief that this terrible doom of the unrepentant dead is equally true." (Rom 2:5-11)

There are numerous opinions and ideas about the details in these verses. Of primary consideration is this fact: *"And if any was not found written in the book of life, he was cast into the lake of fire."* This is the second death, from which there is no escape. It is for eternity, without hope. But, before death, there is hope and grace for those who belong to Jesus, and whose names are found written in the book of life. (John 3:16; 5:24-26; 6:40, 47; 10:9, 14, 28; 11:23; 14:1, 6; 16:33; 20:31; Phil 4:3; Rev 3:5)

21:1-8   The New Heaven and The New Earth. "We come now", says Gaebelein, "to the revelation concerning the final and eternal state of the earth." Says Weidner, "The final judgment has taken place...these last two chapters refer to the eternal Kingdom of God in the new heavens and the new earth...the renewed creation has become the abode of glorified humanity and the tabernacle of God is with redeemed mankind." It would seem as though we must take these things literally, because there is no other way to take them!

John saw *"a new heaven and a new earth"*. Isaiah 65:17 and 66:22 have received their fulfillment! A purified and renovated creation has occurred. (2 Pet 3:7, 10, 12) A new Jerusalem is pictured as *"coming down out of heaven."* The new earth must have a new capital.
(Gal 4:26; Heb 12:22, 11:10)

The new Jerusalem is a holy city, occupied by those *"prepared as a bride beautifully dressed for her husband"*. It is the bride of Christ. (Rev 19:17, 18)

"Now the dwelling of God is with men", thus the ancient promises are fulfilled. (Ex 29:45; Lev 26:11; Ezk 37:27) There will be *"no more death"*, so therefore no more sin, as death is sins result. No death, no mourning. No crying, no violence or oppression. No pain, no misery. The whole order

Revelation

of things caused by the fall, by sin and rebellion which existed in the first creation, have passed away!

See 21:27. Is your name written in *"the Lamb's book of life"*?

In verses 5 and 6 is the proclamation from *"He who was seated on the throne said, I am making everything new!"*. This is a true and trustworthy statement, as it is spoken by *"the Alpha and the Omega, the Beginning and the End"*. (Rev 1:8, 22:13)

"He who overcomes will inherit all this." Another reference that encourages steadfastness of the Believer to persevere until the climax of the present age. (Rev 2:25-28) The ungodly are *"placed in the fiery lake of burning sulphur. This is the second death."*

21:9-27   New Jerusalem Coming Down. The description of the Holy City is glorious to comprehend. There is much to try and understand, but as J. N. Darby said, "The difference of the stones contains details which are above my knowledge." Even so, there are specific references that can be understood.

The city has twelve gates (the twelve tribes of Israel), and twelve foundations (the twelve Apostles). The design of the city may be a cube or pyramid, approximately 1500 miles on each side. A great variety of beautiful stones and precious metals, etc., are used to make or adorn the incredible and awesome structure. (Hag 2:6-9)

There is no temple seen, as *"the Lord God Almighty and the Lamb are its temple"*. Apparently the whole of the heavenly city is the temple. No sun or moon are needed as the *"glory of God gives it light, and the Lamb is its lamp"*. This imperial city receives tribute from the nations and kings of the earth. Who these nations and kings are is a mystery. There is much debate and opinion on these things, only to be understood in a future time. For now, the important understanding is found in 21:27.

Wycliffe rightly concludes, "The vocabulary of man, made for life here, is incapable of truly and adequately depicting what God has prepared for those that love Him!"

22:1-6   The River of Life. These verses are a continuation and a completion of the description of the glory prepared for Believers in the New Jerusalem. *"The river of water of life"* is symbolic of the Holy Spirit, and reflecting on the paradise of Genesis 2:8-10, as well as Ezekiel 47:1-12.

As in the Ezekiel passage there are trees, one in particular, *"the tree of life... yielding twelve crops of fruit, one each month"*.

A continuous supply of nourishment and healing. A better Greek interpretation for "healing" is "health." Healing presupposes disease, while health does not. In the perfect kingdom, where sin is cast out, the nations have no need of healing. The "curse" is no longer present.

The Believers, as servants of the Lord, will *"see His face"* and be identified with Him as *"His name will be on their foreheads"*.

*(*Verse 4*)* They belong absolutely to Him. In this divine place *"there shall be no more night"*. (Rev 21:25) The Apocalypse closes with *"they shall reign forever and ever"*, and *"these words"* are confirmed as *"trustworthy and true"* by the angel in attendance to the Apostle John.

(Beware of Antichrist, the great deceiver, using 22:4 as justification for taking his mark. (Rev 14:9-12)

22:7 - 21   Jesus is Coming. The epilogue; final testimony, invitation, warning, promise and benediction.

"Behold, I am coming soon!" (Acts 1:11) *"I come quickly."* (Rev 1:3; 3:11; 22:12, 20) This refers to the "swiftness" and "speed" of His coming, and does not necessarily mean near at hand. See comments on 2 Peter 3:8-10.

"In verse 7 we are carried back to Revelation 1:3. This command to *'keep the words of the prophecy of this book'* (3:8, 16; 12:17; 14:12) emphasizes a truth we are prone to forget, namely that the prophetic Scriptures have ethical implications. Prophecies and commandments are here bound together." - Wycliffe.

Verses 10 and 11 advise the book is not to be sealed up because it is to be put immediately to use. Let all who believe prepare themselves for His coming.

Revelation

Wycliffe comments, "It is not only true that the troubles of the last days will tend to fix the character of each individual according to the habits already formed, but there will come a time when change is impossible, when no further opportunity will be given for repentance on the one hand, and for apostasy on the other."

The tendency of many people is to become "set in our ways", and to not be acceptable to new information and facts. Verse 11 is a verification of this.

Jesus speaks plainly, in His own name, in verses 12-16. His proclamation is in keeping with all He has done, and will do for those who are His reward and are with Him. *"I will give to everyone according to what he has done."*

It is faith alone that saves a person, but people are rewarded according to their own good works of righteousness.
(James 2:14-17, 26)

"I am the Alpha and the Omega." The same words spoken by God Himself, but this is no reason why Christ cannot use the same declaration of Himself. (Rom 11:36; Col 1:16; Luke 22:66-70)

Furthermore, in verse 16 Jesus declares that He is the *"Root and the Offspring of David, and the bright Morning Star".* He is plainly staking His claim of Messiah to the Jewish people. (John 4:25, 26)

Verse 17 offers an invitation, *"Come!"* It is from the *"Spirit and the Bride".* The Holy Spirit convicts the heart of sin (John 16:8), and the Church, the Bride, offers further testimony and a place to accept the invitation to fellowship with like minded Believers, and partake of the *"free gift of the water of life".*

Lange says, "It is the last full evangelistic tone in the New Testament." It is the invitation given for the last time to the weary and heavy laden (Matt 11:28-30) to come and drink of the water of salvation. Time is about to run out on those who reject the Gospel.

A stern and solemn warning is given in verses 18 and 19. Do not add to, or take away, *"words from this book of prophecy".* The penalty is severe; *"God will take away from him his share in the tree of life and in the holy city which are described in this book".*

Fausset has remarked, "As in the beginning of this book (Rev 1:3) a blessing was promised to the devout, obedient student to it, so now at its close a curse is denounced against those who add to or take away from it."

The reference is to be immediately referred to the book of Revelation, as the whole of the New Testament had not yet been compiled. Irrelevant and trifling interpretation could be included as well.

Jesus concludes with a confirming statement, *"Yes, I am coming soon."*

John offers the benediction of *"Amen. Come Lord Jesus. The grace of the Lord Jesus be with God's people. Amen."*

Without "grace" we are doomed! Praise God for His Grace through His Son, Jesus Christ, the Savior and promised Messiah. Believe in Him, submit to Him, and have everlasting life with Him.

(John 3:16-18, 35, 36)

Amazing grace, how sweet the sound
That sav'd a wretch like me!
I once was lost, but now am found,
Was blind, but now I see.
'Twas grace that taught my heart to fear,
And grace my fears reliev'd;
How precious did that grace appear,
The hour I first believ'd!
Thro' many dangers, toils and snares,
I have already come;
'Tis grace has brought me safe thus far,
And grace will lead me home.

Addendum

One-world Religion Activities at the United Nations
(Preparing for "One World")

There is an alarming rise of ecumenism and moral relativity in the western world. In an age where evangelical Christianity – and for that matter, Judaism – is seen as too "intolerant" or "divisive" for a civilized world, interfaith movements, the New Age Movement, and Unitarian Universalism are gaining in popularity. Nowhere is that more evident than within the United Nations, that seems to ignore Islamic activities and allows evil Islamic rulers to use the UN platform to spew their propaganda and hate.

Influential powers at the United Nations may now be paving the way for the Antichrist. It is imperative to make Christians aware of the powerful New Age influence at the United Nations. The documentation from which this information is based came from official sources: the websites of The Aquarian Age Community(1) and the Lucis Trust(2).

The United Nations (which was started on October 24, 1945) exists as an official Pseudo-governmental body. There are however, scores of advisory committees, boards, and other non-governmental organizations (NGO's) upon which the U.N. relies heavily. The two organizations referenced here are NGO's that provide assistance, advice, and counseling to the U.N. officials and staff. They are the Aquarian Age Community and the Lucis Trust. The Aquarian Age Community (AAC) holds their meetings within a conference room at the United Nations building. How involved is the AAC at the U.N.? Take your answer from the AAC itself:

"We have an informal network at the UN, a humanity underground. It consists of those who are committed, aware, and striving to bring the New World to birth. It consists of people in high places and the patient secretary (?) who has been 30 years with the UN, but lives with the vision and the spirit; of the professionals, and undersecretaries and heads of departments who are acting out the imperatives that their own inner vision gives them. Some few are conscious of the sources of their inspiration; most are not. They are the Karma Yogis of our time - those whose path of spirituality is to achieve through doing - to grow through serving. They are found not only in the secretariat but also in the delegations to the UN, among the diplomats and their staffs, and also among folks like us, representatives of non-governmental organizations around the UN."1

So what does the AAC believe? What is its theology? To what form of "spirituality" do they refer? The AAC is a New Age organization. The only form of divinity they recognize comes from within each person, when they are at "oneness" with everyone and everything else. They practice meditation and astral projection, and accept direction from spirit guides. One of their most revered spirit guides is referred to by many names, and was the spirit guide of Lucis Trust founder Alice Bailey. This spirit guide is called "The Tibetan Master, Djwhal Khul", or sometimes just "The Tibetan Master". The AAC meets regularly at the U.N. and discusses New Age spirituality.

They open their meetings with meditation. One of their purposes as outlined in their mission statements is to "promote the work of the United Nations as it seeks to uplift and improve life on our planet". Another purpose they list is to "cooperate and collaborate with the worldwide community that is actively preparing the way for the reappearance of the World-Teacher – the Christed (Anointed) One, the true Aquarian." 1

They do NOT recognize the deity of Jesus Christ. They believe Jesus was a great teacher, and more in touch with his godhood than most humans are. The AAC believes in evolution – both physical and spiritual. They believe that humans have evolved physically to this point, and the next step in human evolution is spiritual. These people admire Jesus as having been more evolved than most, but do not be confused when they speak of Christ. Be assured that they are not referring to the same Christ of the Bible. If fact, when they refer to "the Christ", they say this:

"From direct experience of the shifting energies, it is possible to recognize that we are progressively moving toward the long awaited Aquarian Age - the Age in which we expect and look for the reappearance of the World Spiritual Teacher. This Great Being has been referred to by such names as the Christ, the Bodhisattva, the Lord Maitreya, and the Imam Mahdi. Many today realize that His interest and concern is not restricted to the field and department of religion, but is concerned with the whole of Life. He is known to be the great Lord of Love and Compassion, the Master of the Masters, the Instructor of the Angels and the "One for Whom all the nations wait." And, this Great Being is also known under such additional titles as the True Aquarian, the Pilgrim, the Healer and the Thinker."1 "Christ is "the embodied soul of all love within our planet". Christ as a Great Initiate appeared on our planet 2,000 years ago and this same great Being will reappear again. He is the only such Teacher who will have been with humanity during two astrological cycles-the Piscean and the Aquarian."

"This time, there will also be an awakening from within many individuals so that the Christ will not just be an outer manifestation, but it is also a great inner happening.

The christ nature which is another way of referring to spiritual love will awaken in humanity. This must happen before there can be the reappearance of the Great Teacher in physical form. He, or She, may return in the field of science or politics or finance, and most likely not in the field of religion. Certainly this Great Being will work in an arena where the highest good for the whole of the planet can be accomplished-where greater numbers of His/Her workers can be found preparing the Way by laboring for the common good." 1

"The reappearance will take place on many different levels. There will be a Great Being who will be recognized as the World Spiritual Teacher. Also, this Great Being will bring a vortex of planetary and cosmic energy that will be available to those who can respond to it, inspiring and strengthening the cause of all that which is Good, True and Beautiful. The reappearance also refers to the expression of the christ or love nature within humanity. It refers to the birth of the christ nature (the soul) within the "cave of the human heart" (the physical plane)." 1

This "great teacher" or "great being" for which the AAC waits will indeed appear. However, unlike the grand personage they describe, the one they describe will be the Antichrist. For further evidence of this, the AAC states that <u>those of us looking for the second coming of our Lord will not recognize the teacher for whom they wait:</u>

"He has been for two thousand years the supreme Head of the Church Invisible, the spiritual Hierarchy, composed of disciples of all faiths. He recognizes and loves those who are not Christian but who retain their allegiance to their Founders--the Buddha, Mohammed, and others. He cares not what the faith is, if the objective is love of God and of humanity. <u>If men look for the Christ Who left His disciples centuries ago they will fail to recognize the Christ Who is in process of returning.</u>"[1]

The AAC also gives us a clue as to the location from which they see the Antichrist originating: "It may interest you to know that the Christ has not yet decided what type of physical vehicle He will employ should He take physical form and work definitely upon the physical plane. He waits to see what nation or group of nations do the most work, and the most convincing work, in preparation for His reappearance." [1]

The AAC sees the United Nations as a great catalyst for bringing about the New World Order and paving the way for the return of their great teacher (Antichrist). For instance, take heed of their words of vision of and for the UN:

"The UN can be a place for education along spiritual lines (within the UN itself and in the world." [1]

"The UN is the largest publisher in the world and it can provide a vast amount of information about the planet and its people." [1]

"The UN should have oversight over all the armaments of the world."[1]

"The UN offers a place for group work; for learning the art of compromise; for breaking down nationalism and fostering a spirit of globalism;..." [1]

"Also, as individuals, we can urge our government to pay its dues so the UN can move forward with its mission, which is essentially a spiritual one: to bring humanity together as a unified center of consciousness." [1]

"Another purpose of the UN concerns education; through changes in education such as introducing school children to the principles and values of the UN (which are inherently spiritual although not religious, per se) children can be assisted in their spiritual development." 1

"Education is key. We should influence the government to teach goodwill in schools. Community access Cable TV programs are also a way to educate the public. We should utilize these means of helping to educate public opinion." 1

"The time has now come when money must be reevaluated and its usefulness channeled into new directions. Until these things are in process of being righted, the return of the Christ is not possible." 1

"In a few short years...the United Nations has succeeded in:

- acquiring a spiritual Initiate at its helm (thus acknowledging increasing perception, unconscious though it may be, on the part of world representatives),

- reorienting the attitudes of even the most recalcitrant delegates to consideration of the Whole, as demonstrated by the policies and actions taken to this end its main bodies,

- establishing branches worldwide that give hope and aid to the masses,

- giving rise to spiritual activities both through NGOs and UN staff, including senior delegates as well as delegates from international organizations such as the World Bank." 1

The AAC is NOT shy about its New Age spiritual agenda, or that of the United Nations' official body. Probably the biggest obstacles to the absolute fulfillment of this New Age agenda are what the AAC views as divisive religions like Judaism and Christianity. Their solution for the UN to overcome these obstacles is as follows:

"...the UN should hold a global conference on the new paradigm and the UN should encourage the spiritual development of its staff members;" 1

"Recognition of the One Humanity can be created through religious unification and realization of the One Divinity." 1

"What is the spiritual purpose of the UN? To find the common ground in all religions and to create practices that unite the spiritual expressions of all cultures". 1

In other words, the AAC envisions one global religion based on their New Age beliefs, that would replace all existing religions – including Christianity. The information presented above is a sampling of information obtained from the AAC that clearly demonstrates their New Age beliefs and their involvement with the United Nations. Their goal of paving the way for the "Christed One" depends on the religious globalization efforts of the UN.

How does the Lucis Trust fit into all this? The Lucis Trust, incorporated originally in New York as the Lucifer Publishing Company, was founded by Alice Bailey – an occultist. Lucis Trust is a United Nations NGO and has been a major player at the recent U.N. summits. Later Assistant Secretary General of the U.N. Robert Muller would credit the creation of his World Core Curriculum for education to the underlying teachings of The Tibetan Master, Djwahl Kuhl via Alice Bailey's writings on the subject.

At one time, the Lucis Trust office in New York was located at 866 United Nations Plaza and it is a member of the Economic and Social Council of the United Nations under a program called "World Goodwill".2

Among the many sponsors of the Lucis Trust are: former U.S. Defense Secretary Robert McNamara, the president of the World Bank, a member of the Rockefeller Foundation, and Thomas Watson (IBM, former ambassador in Moscow). Lucis Trust sponsors the following organizations: UN, Greenpeace Int., Greenpeace USA, Amnesty Int., UNICEF, and many others.

The New Age spirituality that pervades the U.N. is clear. It is also clear that forces are at work to pave the way for the appearance of the Antichrist.

As Christians, we know that we will not know the day or the hour of our Savior's return, and to try to predict such a date is foolhardy at best. However, it is incumbent upon Believers to be aware of the speed with which the forces of Satan are at work in our world -- if for no other reason than to remind us that our time is getting shorter, and we must make the most use of the time left. There is a great harvest of souls to be made, and the harvesters are few. May God grant you wisdom, strength, and courage as you contend for your faith.

1 Taken from the official website of the Aquarian Age Community (sponsored by the U.N.)
2 Taken from the Lucis Trust website

*"**Don't let anyone deceive you in any way,** for that day will not come until the rebellion occurs, and the man of lawlessness is revealed, the man doomed to destruction."* — *2 Thessalonians 2:3*

"And no wonder, for Satan himself masquerades as an angel of light."
-2 Corinthians 11:14

177

Lightning Source UK Ltd.
Milton Keynes UK
UKOW051922141111

182047UK00002B/173/P